106 QUESTIONS CHILDREN ASK ABOUT OUR WORLD

106 Questions Children Ask about Our World

General Editor:
Daryl J. Lucas

Contributors:
David R. Veerman, M.Div.
James C. Galvin, Ed.D.
James C. Wilhoit, Ph.D.
Richard Osborne
Jonathan Farrar

Illustrator:
Lil Crump

Tyndale House Publishers, Inc. Wheaton, Illinois

Visit Tyndale's exciting Web site at www.tyndale.com

Produced for Tyndale by Lightwave Publishing and The Livingstone Corporation. James C. Galvin, David R. Veerman, Daryl J. Lucas, Jonathan Farrar, Livingstone project staff.

Library of Congress Cataloging-in-Publication Data

106 questions children ask about our world / general editor,
    Daryl J. Lucas ; contributors, David R. Veerman . . . [et al.] ; illustrator,
    Lil Crump.
      p. cm.
    ISBN 0-8423-4527-2 (sc : alk. paper)
    1. Nature—Religious aspects—Christianity—Juvenile literature.
    2. Nature—Miscellanea—Juvenile literature. I. Lucas, Daryl.
  II. Veerman, David.
  BT695.5.A18 1998
  230—dc21   97-41761

Printed in the United States of America

04 03 02 01 00 99 98
11 10 9 8 7 6 5 4 3 2 1

CONTENTS

OUTER SPACE

THE BEGINNING AND THE END

INTRODUCTION

What a crazy world we live in! It seems that every day brings change, and with every change comes a new set of questions that catches parents off guard. Of course, children don't see it as "change"—this world today is all they know. But the fact that it's new and changing means that it's new to the parents as well as to the kids. If only moms and dads had time to prepare for the exam. . . .

But kids can't wait while their parents take time to absorb it all. A friend from another country has a different religion. The news reports another earthquake. A new gizmo suddenly seems to be everywhere. Friends, television, days at school, and life itself bring new and puzzling questions every day, and growing up demands that kids get some answers, now.

That is the reason for this book. We collected hundreds of questions children asked about our world, selected the most common and important, and sorted them into categories. If you are a parent of children ages 3 to 10, or if you work with children, you have surely heard questions like these. If not, you soon will.

For every question, we identified relevant Bible passages and then summarized the Bible's application to that question. Study the Scriptures listed with the questions, because the Bible has a lot to say about how we live. It doesn't answer every question directly, but it gives principles that Christians should know and live by.

As you answer your children's questions, keep the following points in mind.

1. "Silly" questions are serious questions. Always take a child's questions seriously. Don't laugh at them. Some questions may sound silly to you, but they're not silly to your child. Be careful not to ridicule your child's ideas.

2. Some questions hide hope or fear. When a child asks, "Can kids be astronauts if they get trained?" (question 96), she's probably hoping to be one herself. She wants to know if she could be an astronaut. Go ahead and address that hope. You could ask follow-up questions such as, "What would you find most exciting about being an astronaut?" or "Why do you ask?" Also take the opportunity to explain how God has a plan for her life and can help her make decisions about her job and career if she will ask him for wisdom.

3. The best answers come from Scripture. The Bible doesn't satisfy every curiosity we have, but it does have principles and guidelines for how we live in our world. We need to be wise, not naive, about the world's dangers. The Bible tells us how to do this, no matter what era of technology we happen to be in. Study the Scriptures listed with each answer, including the Related Verses, for God's timeless wisdom.

4. The best answers avoid theological jargon. Use normal words. Children think in terms of their own experience, so abstract concepts have little meaning to them. As much as possible, talk about *things, events,* and *objects* they can imagine. Give them something to look at in their mind. If they can imagine it, they will understand it.

5. Some questions have no answer. Be careful not to make up an answer when you don't have one and when the Bible is silent. If you don't have an answer, say so. Or suggest that you look for the answer together. If you invent answers, your child will eventually lump the Bible with childhood silliness. Emphasize the truths and guidelines of Scripture that you *do* know. And express trust in God that he does have answers and will reveal them in his own time.

6. Some kids just want to keep asking. Be ready for follow-up questions and be willing to keep talking. Your answer may lead to more questions. That's the mark of a good answer—it makes the child think.

We wrote this book to help you answer kids' questions about living in our world. We sincerely hope and pray it does that.

—Dave Veerman, Jim Galvin, Jim Wilhoit, Daryl Lucas, Rick Osborne, Jon Farrar, Lil Crump

IN THE NEWS

Q: WHY DID GOD PUT LIGHTNING AND THUNDER AND ALL THAT DANGEROUS STUFF IN THE WORLD?

A: God created the world with natural forces that work for our good, and lightning is one of those natural forces. For example, the powerful electrical charge released in lightning makes nitrogen, which we need in the air we breathe. Thunder is simply the sound that lightning makes. Lightning is a good thing, not a bad thing.

But it is also dangerous. Lightning can hurt or kill someone who gets in the way of it. That is why we should not stand outside in a storm when lightning is doing its work.

Almost anything can be dangerous if used in the wrong way or if abused. Even a small rubber band can be dangerous if left on the floor where a baby is crawling. We need to respect nature and natural forces. This means avoiding very dangerous areas and acting wisely.

KEY VERSE: *He gives his sunlight to both the evil and the good, and he sends rain on the just and on the unjust, too. (Matthew 5:45)*

RELATED QUESTIONS: *Why does lightning hit people? Do thunder and lightning mean that God is angry?*

NOTE TO PARENTS: *People sometimes flaunt natural laws and act irresponsibly (like building homes on a floodplain, on a fault line, or near a volcano). The Bible says that "fear of the Lord is the beginning of knowledge" (Proverbs 1:7). When we live our lives in cooperation with God's principles and laws of creation, we are using wisdom.*

Q: WHY DOES GOD KILL NATURE WITH FOREST FIRES?

A: Forest fires don't kill nature. They are part of the life cycle that God built into our world. Raging forest fires can destroy many thousands of trees and wildlife. But forest fires also help life continue. For example, they burn away dead growth and open seed pods, such as those of jack pines, which can't be opened any other way. Forest fires are a little like lightning— they may be dangerous, but they do important work.

Some forest fires start naturally, and some are started by people. We should not try to start forest fires just to destroy property. And we should try to keep them from damaging property or endangering people's lives. But some fires start naturally, and we know now that they are necessary. This is just part of God's plan for us and our world.

KEY VERSES: *Then God said, "Let the land burst forth with every sort of grass and seed-bearing plant. And let there be trees that grow seed-bearing fruit. The seeds will then produce the kinds of plants and trees from which they came." And so it was. The land was filled with seed-bearing plants and trees, and their seeds produced plants and trees of like kind. And God saw that it was good. (Genesis 1:11-12)*

RELATED VERSES: *Psalm 83:14; Psalm 96:12; James 3:5*

RELATED QUESTIONS: *Why do forest fires happen? How do forest fires start? How do forest fires stop?*

NOTE TO PARENTS: *Whenever your children ask about fire, be careful not to overplay fear to keep them from it. Fire can be used for good purposes, even though it is dangerous. Simply teach them to respect these dangers, to use fire responsibly, and to handle it wisely.*

Q: WHY DO FLOODS AND HURRICANES KILL INNOCENT PEOPLE?

A: Most floods, and all hurricanes, are natural disasters that can't be prevented. They are simply events that happen when water strikes with great force (for example, from storms at sea, heavy rains, or melting snow). The forces of nature go to work, and those forces are very powerful.

Sometimes people die in these natural disasters because they have not listened to a warning. Some live too near the water and in areas that flood easily. Some ignore storm warnings and stay in the path of danger when they should leave. Some even try to get *close* to a powerful storm, risking their lives because they think it will be exciting. Too many people die in floods and hurricanes because they are foolish.

But others die through no fault of their own; they are in the wrong place at the wrong time. It is not because God overlooked them; it is because we live in a broken world. We have suffering and death because of sin.

Deaths from floods and hurricanes are tragedies. That is why we need to be wise and do what we can to avoid unnecessary risks. As long as we have sin in this world we will have these dangers, and we need to avoid them.

KEY VERSE: *Anyone who listens to my teaching and obeys me is wise, like a person who builds a house on solid rock. (Matthew 7:24)*

RELATED VERSES: *Matthew 7:25-27*

RELATED QUESTIONS: *Why do big floods happen? Why do tornadoes happen? Why do hurricanes happen? How fast do tornadoes turn? Why don't people go before their house gets flooded? Why do floods and tornadoes kill people?*

Q: WHY DOES GOD SEND EARTHQUAKES?

A: Like hurricanes, earthquakes are a natural part of the way the earth works. Huge pieces of the earth's surface, called tectonic plates, are shifting and rubbing against each other all the time. Sometimes their movements release great amounts of energy stored up in the friction between them. The release of this energy produces an earthquake. It is not that God sends earthquakes so much as that they happen as part of the world God has made.

Earthquakes can do a lot of damage to buildings and other structures not made to handle the mighty rumblings and shocks. If possible, people who live in earthquake areas should have homes built with earthquakes in mind. They should also plan how they will get to safety the next time an earthquake happens. This is simply an example of planning wisely and being careful.

KEY VERSE: *When the earth quakes and its people live in turmoil, I am the one who keeps its foundations firm. (Psalm 75:3)*

RELATED QUESTIONS: *How do earthquakes happen? Why do earthquakes have to happen? Why do only certain areas get earthquakes?*

NOTE TO PARENTS: *If you live in an area prone to earthquakes, teach your children what to do in the event of a tremor. Be familiar with basic safety steps— including where to go and what not to do—and explain them to your children. You can even make a game of practicing them!*

Q: WHY DO PEOPLE DIE IN HOT WEATHER?

A: Temperatures over 100 degrees Fahrenheit (35 degrees Celsius) put a lot of stress on the human body. In hot weather, bodies need more water than normal because they lose water more quickly. Older people and those who are sick suffer the most, because their bodies are not as strong as younger, healthier people. Most of the people who die in hot weather become overheated because they can't get cooled off. If they would go to a cooler place or to a building with air-conditioning, they could cool off.

This is one way people can look out for each other. If you have older relatives, make sure they have a way to get cool on a really hot day.

KEY VERSE: *O God, you are my God; I earnestly search for you. My soul thirsts for you; my whole body longs for you in this parched and weary land where there is no water. (Psalm 63:1)*

RELATED VERSES: *Deuteronomy 8:15; Job 6:17-18; Isaiah 32:1-2*

RELATED QUESTIONS: *What is the hottest place in the world? What is the coldest place in the world?*

NOTE TO PARENTS: *Children tend to think of themselves as invulnerable and often don't know the dangers that high heat can pose. Make sure your kids know how to handle themselves in hot weather. They should drink plenty of fluids, try to stay cool, stay out of the sun, and limit their exercise.*

Q: WHO FEEDS PEOPLE WHO DON'T HAVE ENOUGH TO EAT?

6

A: Although there is plenty of food in the world, thousands of people go hungry every day. Maybe they live far from food or they just don't have money to buy food.

Many people who care about this work hard to feed those who don't have enough to eat. This is the main purpose of many relief organizations. Some government agencies, churches, and other organizations also help. If you know of a hungry family, you could take them a bag of groceries or a special meal. You could also support the work of a Christian organization that is working with the poor. Some people sponsor children through agencies; some donate money; others take food to food pantries; and some donate time at homeless shelters, soup kitchens, and other places that help poor people.

KEY VERSES: *Suppose you see a brother or sister who needs food or clothing, and you say, "Well, good-bye and God bless you; stay warm and eat well"—but then you don't give that person any food or clothing. What good does that do? (James 2:15-16)*

RELATED VERSES: *Proverbs 28:27; Romans 12:8-9*

RELATED QUESTIONS: *Why don't we help people who don't have enough to eat? Why don't some people in the world have enough to eat? Why aren't people generous to give food to people who don't have enough to eat? Why can't we give our food to hungry people?*

NOTE TO PARENTS: *It is good to get involved as a family to help meet the needs of the poor. It helps people in a tangible way and also shows God's love to them. Consider options available to you through your church or another organization that you trust.*

Q: WHY DO PEOPLE COMMIT CRIMES?

7

A: The main reason people commit crimes is that they are selfish. They want what others have and take it by force. Another big reason is anger. People get so angry that they lose their temper and do things that they would not normally do. Both selfishness and uncontrolled anger are sin.

Crime happens when people get cut off from God and his love. Some people do not know God at all and do not know that they can trust him to take care of them. Some people know him but lose touch with him, then fail to trust and obey him. God's way is for us to know him, to ask and trust him for the things we need, and then to love and help others. If everyone did things God's way all the time, crime would never happen. That is why we need to trust God to provide for us instead of selfishly trying to get what we want regardless of how it affects others.

KEY VERSE: *When they refused to acknowledge God, he abandoned them to their evil minds and let them do things that should never be done. (Romans 1:28)*

RELATED VERSES: *Proverbs 4:16-17; Romans 1:29-32; 3:23; Ephesians 4:26-27, 31-32*

NOTE TO PARENTS: *It is important to teach children to talk their way through conflicts with others instead of forcing their way by hitting, screaming, or threatening. On the playground, at school, and among siblings, they will get into conflicts of will every day. Most things are not worth fighting for. It is OK to try to persuade; it is not OK to use force on those who disagree. Remind them that they can control their temper (Proverbs 12:16).*

Q: WHAT ARE CRIME WAVES?

JASON'S
IMAGINATION

8

A: You know what a wave is—it's a whole bunch of water moving in the same direction all at once. A crime wave is a whole bunch of crime all happening at once.

Crime waves often start when many people think they can get away with their crimes. For example, an upsetting event happens, and a mob of people react in some criminal way, like breaking store windows and stealing the merchandise. Or there is a natural disaster that leaves stores open and unprotected, and local people loot them, thinking that they won't get caught. Or a new crime comes along, like doing drugs, and many people do it.

Don't be fooled by the popularity of a crime wave. Wrong is wrong, no matter how many people do it. A crime is a crime, even if the police never catch anyone doing it. It is not possible to get away with a crime, because "you can't ignore God and get away with it. You will always reap what you sow!" (Galatians 6:7).

KEY VERSE: *My child, if sinners entice you, turn your back on them! (Proverbs 1:10)*

RELATED VERSES: *Proverbs 1:11-19; 4:14; Matthew 27:16*

RELATED QUESTIONS: *Why are there crime waves? How does crime happen? Why is crime worse in some places?*

Q: WHY IS THE WORLD SO VIOLENT AND EVIL?

9

A: Sin is the root cause of all evil. Because people sin, the world is filled with sin and evil. It has been this way since Adam and Eve's first sin. In fact, God flooded the world in Noah's day because of violence and evil. These things are not new.

In some ways it may seem that violence is worse today than in the past. Weapons are more destructive than ever before. There are more guns and knives and more ways of hurting people than ever before. As these weapons get more powerful, so does the power to hurt others.

But in reality, violence and evil come out of evil hearts that are separated from God, and the world has always had that. As long as people rebel against God, we will have violence and evil in the world.

KEY VERSE: *Don't let evil get the best of you, but conquer evil by doing good. (Romans 12:21)*

RELATED VERSES: *Genesis 6:11-13; 1 John 5:19*

RELATED QUESTIONS: *What percent of the world is violent? Why do people do bad things? Is Satan the only cause for evil? Why are there bad things in the world? How come people are doing so many bad things in the world? Why do they show so many guns on the news?*

NOTE TO PARENTS: *When your children ask a question like this, make sure they get a balanced view. Talk about all the good that is happening in the world. Many believers are telling others about Christ, helping to relieve suffering through health care, serving as missionaries, praying for leaders, and working behind the scenes to achieve good. God has not abandoned our world.*

Q: WHY ARE THERE SO MANY ACCIDENTS AND PEOPLE GETTING KILLED?

10

A: Because of sin in the world. When God created the world, everything was perfect. But when the first people disobeyed God, sin threw things out of order. This is what it means to say we live in a *fallen world*. It is full of dangers. If it weren't for sin, we would not have suffering or death at all.

Some of our own creations have also brought new dangers. The fact that we can go faster in cars and planes means that accidents can have bigger and worse results. People also have lots of accidents when they are in a hurry. As they rush from place to place, they run into others.

It is important to be careful. This means looking both ways before crossing streets, watching where you are going, wearing seat belts, and using common sense. As long as accidents happen in this world, we must be careful.

KEY VERSE: *A prudent person foresees the danger ahead and takes precautions. The simpleton goes blindly on and suffers the consequences. (Proverbs 27:12)*

RELATED VERSES: *Proverbs 1:32-33; Luke 13:4-5*

RELATED QUESTIONS: *How come the news is so boring? Why don't they just put in the newspaper what they were going to put on TV?*

NOTE TO PARENTS: *Whenever you pray with your children about God protecting them, ask God for the wisdom and common sense they need to live safely. This helps them remember that they have a role to play in staying safe.*

CULTURES
AND
COUNTRIES

11

A: Some names sound strange to you, but they sound fine in the countries that have them. Names have meaning inside their own cultures. For example, we might think that a name like Botswana or Bosnia-Herzegovina sounds weird because we don't live there and don't know what the name means. But in those countries, New York, Vancouver, Saskatchewan, and Alaska probably sound silly too.

KEY VERSE: *That area, too, was once considered the land of the Rephaites, though the Ammonites referred to them as Zamzummites. (Deuteronomy 2:20)*

RELATED VERSES: *Judges 12:5-6; Colossians 3:11; Revelation 5:9-13*

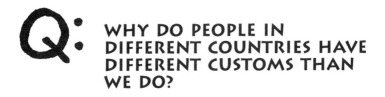

Q: WHY DO PEOPLE IN DIFFERENT COUNTRIES HAVE DIFFERENT CUSTOMS THAN WE DO?

12

A: One reason is that many years ago there was very little communication among countries that were far apart. People living in Africa, for example, didn't know anything about people living in Asia, and people in Australia didn't know about people in America. The people in each country developed their own way of doing things without knowing how others around the world were doing them.

Another reason for many of the differences is climate. In places where the weather is always hot, people will dress and eat in ways that make sense in hot areas. Eskimos dress in furs and eat lots of fish because that's what they need to wear and that's what kind of food is available in their climate.

Always show respect for people who are not like you. It is a simple way to honor and learn to enjoy the marvelous variety of people and nations God has made.

KEY VERSE: *I try to find common ground with everyone so that I might bring them to Christ. (1 Corinthians 9:22)*

RELATED VERSE: *1 Peter 2:17*

RELATED QUESTION: *Why are people in other countries different?*

NOTE TO PARENTS: *Be sure to distinguish between moral issues and cultural ones. It is wrong to steal or hate, no matter what your culture is. But differences in dress, food, language, music, special celebrations, and even the way a family operates are not wrong. Speak positively of these differences.*

Q: DO PEOPLE KEEP THEIR CULTURE WHEN THEY MOVE TO A DIFFERENT COUNTRY?

13

A: At first they do. In fact, people who move from one country to another often try hard to keep the customs and traditions of their home country. But it is difficult to do, because few of the people around them live the same way, and it takes a big group of people all living the same way to support a culture.

For example, if the people want to speak their native language, they have to talk with others who also speak their language. If they want to eat the food of their homeland, they need to know where they can buy the ingredients. If they celebrate the holidays they grew up with, they may be the only ones doing so.

In most families that move to another country or culture, this is a real struggle. People like that need all the hospitality and welcoming they can get from friends and neighbors.

KEY VERSE: *Don't forget to show hospitality to strangers, for some who have done this have entertained angels without realizing it! (Hebrews 13:2)*

RELATED VERSES: *Genesis 12:1; Romans 12:13; 1 Peter 4:9*

RELATED QUESTIONS: *Why do people immigrate? How could Adam and Eve's children cross the sea to North America?*

NOTE TO PARENTS: *Some children who move from one country to another will treasure the habits and customs of the country they left. Other children will more readily adapt to the customs and habits of their new homeland. Usually this is a matter of personality and disposition. A parent should guide each child through the trauma of moving in the ways that are appropriate for that child. Be sensitive to the different types of personalities and how each person reacts to moving.*

Q: WHY DO PEOPLE HAVE TO SPEAK DIFFERENT LANGUAGES?

14

A: It all started at a place called Babel in Babylonia, where Iraq is today. During the time of Adam and Eve and Noah, everyone in the world spoke the same language. But shortly after Noah and his family emerged from the ark, the people of the world gathered together to build a tower as a monument to their own greatness. They had completely forgotten about God. So God caused their language to divide into dialects. God changed the languages to confuse the people so they wouldn't finish building the Tower of Babel. People who spoke the same language stayed together, moved away, and settled in different areas all over the world. Ever since then, languages have been part of what makes countries different from each other. And even within countries, different ethnic groups often speak different languages.

KEY VERSES: *In that way, the Lord scattered them all over the earth; and that ended the building of the city. That is why the city was called Babel, because it was there that the Lord confused the people by giving them many languages, thus scattering them across the earth. (Genesis 11:8-9)*

RELATED QUESTIONS: *Why do people in different countries speak different? Why are there so many different kinds of languages? Why can't there just be one language?*

Q: WHY DO SOME FAMILIES SPEAK MORE THAN ONE LANGUAGE?

15

A: Some families live in parts of the world where all people speak more than one language. Many Europeans, especially those in small countries, are in this situation. People in Germany, for example, live quite close to people in France and England, and they will probably need to speak to English speakers and French speakers many times throughout their lives. So as they grow up, they learn to speak English and French as well as German. That's three languages right there.

Some people live in countries that have two or more official languages. Canada has two—English and French. Switzerland has three—French, German, and Italian. In countries like these, people usually speak the language most common to their area.

Some people live in cultures where they did not grow up. They have had to learn a new language so they can talk to the people in that land. This is what happens when people come to North America from Mexico, for example, or when people move from North America to Switzerland.

Many missionaries need to learn another language so they can tell people about God in their own language.

KEY VERSE: *Then Eliakim son of Hilkiah, Shebna, and Joah said to the king's representative, "Please speak to us in Aramaic, for we understand it well. Don't speak in Hebrew, for the people on the wall will hear." (2 Kings 18:26)*

RELATED VERSES: *Daniel 7:14; Acts 2:6*

RELATED QUESTIONS: *Why do some people have to speak two languages? What was the first language ever spoken on the earth? What language did Goliath speak? What language did Jesus speak?*

Q: WHY DO PEOPLE IN OTHER COUNTRIES EAT DIFFERENT FOOD?

16

A: People choose what foods to eat for many reasons. Sometimes they eat the foods that they can get easily and that don't cost very much money. A rice farmer, for example, probably would eat a lot of rice. Some foods are very expensive because they have to be grown a long way away or because a certain food is very scarce.

Some foods are chosen because of culture and habit. In some countries, the people have learned to enjoy eating very spicy foods. In other countries, everyone likes fish. And in still other countries, people eat a lot of meat and potatoes. What people eat is a matter of tradition, habit, and personal taste.

KEY VERSES: *Every one of these depends on you to give them their food as they need it. When you supply it, they gather it. You open your hand to feed them, and they are satisfied. (Psalm 104:27-28)*

RELATED VERSE: *Isaiah 25:6*

RELATED QUESTIONS: *Why do some people like sweet and sour or spicy foods? Why do people in different countries eat different foods for feasts?*

NOTE TO PARENTS: *A fun way to help your children learn about and be more accepting of other cultures is to introduce them to different ethnic foods. Take them to an ethnic restaurant, make a meal from an ethnic cookbook, or invite a friend to show you how to make a favorite ethnic dish.*

Q: IN OTHER COUNTRIES, WHY DO PEOPLE BURP ALOUD AFTER MEALS?

17

A: In some countries, burping aloud after a meal shows that you enjoyed the meal. In other countries, it is more polite to say something nice about the meal instead of burping. Different groups of people have different ways of life. It's a good idea to show respect for the people when you travel to another country. Find out which of your behaviors may offend others. That way you can try hard to avoid embarrassing yourself and your hosts.

KEY VERSES: *In those days it was the custom in Israel for anyone transferring a right of purchase to remove his sandal and hand it to the other party. This publicly validated the transaction. So the other family redeemer drew off his sandal as he said to Boaz, "You buy the land." (Ruth 4:7-8)*

RELATED VERSE: *1 Peter 2:17*

RELATED QUESTIONS: *How come in other countries it's all right to burp aloud? Why, when little babies burp, parents say, "Good girl/boy!" but when they get bigger and burp, parents get mad? How come some people in different countries eat with their mouths open and without forks? Why don't people in some countries use tables?*

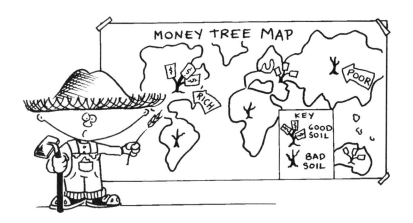

18

A:

Some countries are very rich and others very poor for many reasons. Wealthy countries often have many natural resources (such as oil, gold, rich fisheries, or tourist attractions) that bring them great wealth. They also have economic systems that reward people for making and selling goods and services; they attract buyers with the things they make and sell. And they have laws that protect people from being cheated.

Other countries don't have these things, and that makes them poor. Perhaps they don't have the natural resources that people want to buy. Or perhaps they have the resources, but the economic system makes it hard for people to sell them or for buyers to buy them. Also, some countries have been hurt by war, hurricanes, earthquakes, famines, or other tragedies.

It takes time and cooperation for a country to change from being poor to being rich. Everyone has to work together and support free trade. Everyone has to make rules and keep them. That is one of the ways God rewards people who abide by his laws—obeying the laws keeps things orderly. This is just another example of God's love at work. When we follow God's principles, life works better.

KEY VERSE: *Hard workers have plenty of food; playing around brings poverty. (Proverbs 28:19)*

RELATED VERSES: *Job 12:23; Proverbs 28:15-16; Luke 1:52-53*

RELATED QUESTIONS: *Why are some countries so big and others so small? Why do people in some countries go barefoot and in others they wear shoes? Why can't people wear shorts instead of business suits? Why do some people wear sandals and other people wear shoes?*

Q: WHY IS THERE A McDONALD'S IN ALMOST EVERY COUNTRY?

19

A: Some companies, like McDonald's and Coca-Cola, can be found in many places around the world because they have worked hard to sell their products in those places. They have hired people to set up factories, stores, or distributors in other countries. They have signed contracts with other companies to help them. These companies keep doing this until it seems they have products in almost every country.

Another reason is communication among people around the world. Television, E-mail, the Internet, long-distance telephone connections, and air travel allow people to know a lot about those who live a long way away from them. They learn about other people's customs, products, food, and stores. Some decide to open a branch store in a faraway town. Modern technology has made it easier than ever to do business all over the world.

KEY VERSE: *Judah and Israel traded for your wares, offering wheat from Minnith, early figs, honey, oil, and balm. (Ezekiel 27:17)*

RELATED VERSES: *Ezekiel 27:1-36; Luke 12:16-19*

RELATED QUESTION: *Why are some things the same in almost every country?*

Q: I DON'T GET IT—WHY ARE PEOPLE PREJUDICED?

JESUS LOVES THE LITTLE CHILDREN,
ALL THE CHILDREN OF THE WORLD...

20

A: The biggest reason for prejudice is fear of people who are different. People tend to fear what they don't know or understand, including other people or their customs. People also tend to think badly of people and customs that they don't understand. People become prejudiced when they believe false ideas about what others are like.

We do not need to fear variety in the way people cook, dress, and talk. We need to appreciate these differences and not judge or criticize people just because they do not do these things our way.

Some people also believe—wrongly—that certain kinds of people are better or more important than others. This is called *racism*. People who have this perspective don't realize that God created *all* people in his image. Every person who has ever been born is equally important and valuable. No one is better or deserving of superior treatment.

Jesus wants us to love and respect others, even if we don't know or understand them. We should not think badly of people just because we don't understand them. We should not be prejudiced.

KEY VERSE: *God does not show favoritism. (Romans 2:11)*

RELATED VERSES: *Acts 10:34; Galatians 3:28*

RELATED QUESTIONS: *Why don't some people like people who are different from them? If Adam and Eve are the father and mother of everyone on earth, then why isn't everyone your brother or sister?*

NOTE TO PARENTS: *Children learn prejudice by watching others show it; few parents or others actively teach it. We need to be careful to not use prejudiced language, tell prejudiced jokes, or avoid people for prejudiced reasons.*

RELIGION

Q: WHY DOES THE WORLD HAVE DIFFERENT RELIGIONS?

21

A: Various religions exist for many different reasons. Most cultures know about God, but many that don't know him have tried to explain him in their own ways; they have formed their own religions.

Many people do not want to believe that there is only one way to God, so they start their own way and try to get others to join them. All of those people need to hear about God's love for them and about Jesus' dying for them.

Christianity also has many different *denominations*. A denomination is a group of churches. Some of these groups formed because the people were all from a certain country and culture or spoke a certain language (for example, German Baptists or Swedish Covenant). Other denominations exist because they hold their church services differently from others or believe in expressing their faith in a specific way.

The Bible tells us, however, that Jesus Christ is the *only* way to God. Christians may go to many different churches that speak different languages or have certain types of services as long as their beliefs and worship center on Christ and God's Word. All Christians should love and appreciate each other and work together despite their differences.

KEY VERSE: *Do not worship any other gods besides me. (Exodus 20:3)*

RELATED VERSES: *Exodus 20:4-6; John 14:6; Acts 17:16-34*

NOTE TO PARENTS: *When children focus on what is "wrong" with how other Christians believe or worship, redirect their attention to their own lives. Their energy should be spent on becoming like Christ, not on correcting others.*

Q: WHAT KIND OF HOLY BOOKS DO PEOPLE OF OTHER RELIGIONS HAVE?

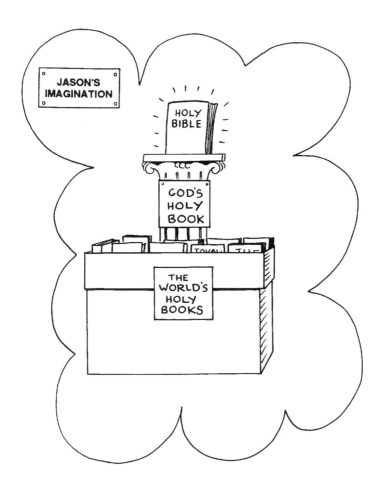

22

A: Many religions have books of instructions or books that help people understand their own religion. Most of these religions have many, many books, not just one. These books explain the beliefs and practices of these religions.

In some ways, this is similar to how Christians use the Bible, but the Bible is also unique. The Bible has many prophecies, or predictions of the future, that have come true exactly as predicted. It also tells of many, many places and events that archaeologists have discovered to be true and accurate. Other "holy books" don't survive all these kinds of tests. The more we learn about the past, the more we learn that we can trust what the Bible says.

KEY VERSE: *Philip went off to look for Nathanael and told him, "We have found the very person Moses and the prophets wrote about! His name is Jesus, the son of Joseph from Nazareth." (John 1:45)*

RELATED VERSES: *Deuteronomy 18:20; Joshua 1:7-8; Revelation 22:8-9*

RELATED QUESTIONS: *Why do people of other religions make holy books? Why do people of other religions think their books are holy books?*

Q: DOES GOD LOVE PEOPLE WHO DON'T PRAY?

SO I WAS THINKING, LORD, IF YOU DROPPED A BILLION STICKY NOTES ALL OVER THE WORLD REMINDING PEOPLE TO PRAY, **THAT** WOULD GET THEIR ATTENTION!

23

A: God loves all people, even those who do not love him. The Bible tells of some unbelieving kings who prayed and to whom God listened. God is delighted whenever someone honors him, calls out to him, or expresses a need for him. And he invites people to come to him because he loves them; his love does not depend on whether or not a person prays.

But that does not mean that God loves everything that people do. Just because God loves people does not make all people right or good in his sight. Having a relationship with Jesus gives a person a relationship with God that not just anyone can have.

That is why God wants us to pray. It allows us to enjoy our relationship with God, to benefit from his friendship, and to see him work in our life.

KEY VERSE: *Then they cried out to the Lord, Jonah's God. "O Lord," they pleaded, "don't make us die for this man's sin. And don't hold us responsible for his death, because it isn't our fault. O Lord, you have sent this storm upon him for your own good reasons." (Jonah 1:14)*

RELATED VERSES: *Psalm 17:1; Jeremiah 29:13; Acts 17:23, 27-31*

RELATED QUESTION: *If Hindus believe in many gods and Buddhists don't believe in any god, how can they live in the same country?*

Q: WHY DO PEOPLE WORSHIP IDOLS INSTEAD OF GOD?

24

A: Idols are simply pictures or statues of imaginary gods. Actually, most people who have idols don't worship the idols but the gods they represent. Some people, however, think that an idol itself can help them.

People want to believe in things that they can see and touch, so they make things they can see. But we cannot see God because God is spirit. As Christians, we do not make or worship idols because idols take our attention away from worshiping the one true God.

KEY VERSE: *No one has ever seen God. But his only Son, who is himself God, is near to the Father's heart; he has told us about him. (John 1:18)*

RELATED VERSES: *Exodus 20:3-4; Psalm 135:15-18; Isaiah 44:9-11*

RELATED QUESTIONS: *What's an idol? What are idols made of? Why do some people pray to objects? Why do people in other countries worship different idols?*

Q: WHY IS BEING GOOD NOT ENOUGH TO GET SOMEONE INTO HEAVEN?

25

A: It is impossible to be good enough to get into heaven. Every person sins, and even one sin is too many for heaven. Heaven is perfect because God is perfect—there is no sin at all in God's presence. A person would have to be perfect to get into heaven.

That is why we need Jesus. Only Jesus can accept us into God's presence by forgiving our sin.

We are each like a pane of glass in a window. If even one tiny corner of it is broken, it is broken. We need a miracle to make us whole again. We need to believe in Jesus and invite him to save us. Then we can have our sins forgiven and be ready for heaven.

KEY VERSE: *As the Scriptures say, "No one is good—not even one." (Romans 3:10)*

RELATED VERSES: *Psalm 14:1-3; Isaiah 1:18; Romans 3:9-18*

RELATED QUESTIONS: *If you did everything right and you were really nice to people, would you go to heaven? Why do people think that even if you're a good person that's not enough to get you to heaven?*

WARS
AND
RUMORS
OF WAR

Q: WHY DO COUNTRIES FIGHT WARS WITH EACH OTHER?

26

A: A war is fought when countries disagree and can't work out their problems by talking together. Sometimes a war will begin when both countries want the same thing, like a certain piece of land. Instead of talking it out, they fight. Other times, a war will begin when one country wants to take over another country.

God wants us to love others and try to get along with others. Many wars could be avoided if everyone followed God's instructions for loving others. And if each of us chooses to love God and others, we can prevent fights and make the world a little more peaceful.

KEY VERSES: *What is causing the quarrels and fights among you? Isn't it the whole army of evil desires at war within you? You want what you don't have, so you scheme and kill to get it. You are jealous for what others have, and you can't possess it, so you fight and quarrel to take it away from them. And yet the reason you don't have what you want is that you don't ask God for it. (James 4:1-2)*

RELATED VERSES: *Psalm 27:3; Proverbs 30:33; Matthew 24:6; James 4:2-3*

RELATED QUESTIONS: *What is the point of having war if all you're doing is risking getting yourself killed? Why can't people stop fighting wars? Why do men go to war and not ladies? How come so many people in the world go to war? Why does God let people shoot each other?*

Q: WHY DO DICTATORS PUSH PEOPLE AROUND SO MUCH?

27

A: Dictators push people around because they like to have power and control over others. One of the most common sins that people commit is to use power to force people to do things their way. Because dictators are in control of everything in the country, they have a lot of power. Pushing people around is their way of abusing that power. Dictators who abuse their power are evil, and God will punish them in the end.

The Bible teaches us that the proper way to lead others is to serve them and put their interests ahead of your own. Whenever you get a chance to be in charge, even of younger brothers or sisters, think of what is best for them and do the fun things they want to do.

KEY VERSE: *When the wicked are in authority, sin increases. But the godly will live to see the tyrant's downfall. (Proverbs 29:16)*

RELATED VERSES: *Proverbs 28:2, 15; 29:2, 4; Isaiah 10:1*

RELATED QUESTIONS: *What are dictatorships? What do dictators do? Why do dictators tell you what to do? Why didn't God kill Hitler? If Hitler knew he was going to be mean, why did he want to govern Germany? Why isn't there a world leader?*

NOTE TO PARENTS: *Parental authority is the first leadership example that children have. Teach them to lead others by demonstrating service-motivated leadership.*

Q: WHY DO COUNTRIES HAVE ARMIES, NAVIES, AND AIR FORCES?

28

A: It is true that some countries have armies, navies, and air forces mainly so they can attack others. But most countries have armed forces only as a defense against invasion. Their forces protect the country from other countries that might want to go to war against them.

In some countries armed forces can also help in peacetime. The soldiers are used to keep order inside the country during protests and riots, and to rescue and help people during natural disasters like floods and hurricanes.

It is important to honor those who risk their lives to protect us. Most countries do this by setting aside a Memorial Day, Remembrance Day, or another holiday for people to remember the people in their armed forces. Remember to show your appreciation the next time this holiday comes around. They are "authorities sent by God to help you."

KEY VERSE: *The authorities are sent by God to help you. But if you are doing something wrong, of course you should be afraid, for you will be punished. The authorities are established by God for that very purpose, to punish those who do wrong. (Romans 13:4)*

RELATED VERSES: *Deuteronomy 20:1; Psalm 20:7; Amos 1:3-15; Romans 13:1-7*

RELATED QUESTIONS: *Why doesn't someone take away all the guns and tell people to love and live in peace instead? Why doesn't the government say, "No abortions, no killing, and no wars—share!"? Why do people even make weapons?*

Q: WHY ARE NUCLEAR WEAPONS EVEN AROUND?

29

A: Nuclear weapons were invented during World War II to gain an advantage over the Axis powers (Germany, Japan, and Italy). The government of the United States hired scientists to build a bomb that would be so powerful that the Japanese would have to surrender.

Because these weapons can kill hundreds of thousands of people at once, people all over the world have been working to get rid of them. They feel that we will only destroy ourselves if we use them.

Others know that these weapons make them powerful, so they work to keep the ones they have, or they make new ones. They feel that they would be defenseless without nuclear weapons.

This is just one reason God commands us to be kind, to forgive, and to return cruelty with kindness. Whenever we allow conflicts to escalate, or get worse, we build bigger weapons and do even more terrible things. God's way is better.

KEY VERSES: *When they refused to acknowledge God, he abandoned them to their evil minds and let them do things that should never be done. Their lives became full of every kind of wickedness, sin, greed, hate, envy, murder, fighting, deception, malicious behavior, and gossip. (Romans 1:28-29)*

RELATED VERSES: *Proverbs 3:25-26; 15:1*

RELATED QUESTIONS: *Why do people want to make weapons to destroy the world? Why do countries have nuclear weapons?*

NOTE TO PARENTS: *The basic principles that help avoid war are the same ones that help brothers and sisters get along. Peace starts at home.*

Q: WHY DO SOME COUNTRIES SPLIT APART?

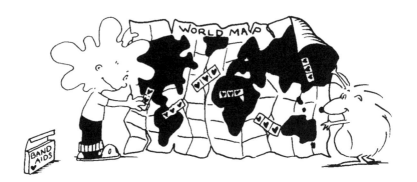

30

A:

Usually countries split apart when a group of people within the country wants to rule itself. It does not want to be part of the larger country anymore. Why would a group want to break away like that? Because different groups of people have different ways of life. People want to govern themselves, and certain groups don't want to be governed by other groups that have different ways of life. Sometimes groups get forced together under the same government against their will, such as in the former Soviet Union. Eventually the people's desire to govern themselves can cause the country to split.

KEY VERSES: *And I have provided a permanent homeland for my people Israel, a secure place where they will never be disturbed. It will be their own land where wicked nations won't oppress them as they did in the past, from the time I appointed judges to rule my people. And I will keep you safe from all your enemies. (2 Samuel 7:10-11)*

RELATED VERSES: *Mark 13:7; Luke 19:14*

RELATED QUESTIONS: *How come countries break away from their old country and become a new country? How come two countries become one country? When two countries join together, do they start their age all over again?*

NOTE TO PARENTS: *It is important to teach our children to respect the will and desires of others, and a brother-and-sister relationship is a good place for them to start. If a brother or sister says, "Stop teasing me," or "Please stop tickling me," or "Stop crowding me," then the other should know that he or she must stop. Make respect for others a basic rule in your house.*

Q: IS GOD HAPPY FOR ONE COUNTRY AND SAD FOR THE OTHER AT THE END OF A WAR?

31

A: God is saddened by all sin and death. In most wars, nobody wins. People from both sides are hurt and killed. Property is destroyed. Countries, cities, neighborhoods, and families are torn apart. God is not happy with any of it. He is sad about all the destruction caused by sin, including war.

But sometimes God does send war as a punishment for evil. In the Old Testament we read that some nations suffered in wars as a punishment for their sins against others. And sometimes war seems to be the only way to stop an evil dictator or an evil government. But that doesn't mean that God is happy to see nations go to war. He much prefers that people obey him, get along with each other, and avoid war altogether.

KEY VERSE: *The Lord will settle international disputes. All the nations will beat their swords into plowshares and their spears into pruning hooks. All wars will stop, and military training will come to an end. (Micah 4:3)*

RELATED VERSES: *Amos 5:6-7, 14-15*

RELATED QUESTIONS: *Who started World War I and II? If God loves the world, why do wars happen? How come wars are still going on in the world? Why don't people help people from other countries and give to them, instead of fighting them?*

LEADERS
AND
POLITICS

Q: WHAT ARE POLITICS?

32

A: *Politics* is the word we use to describe governing or ruling. Politics is when people deal with one another in government. It includes trying to persuade someone else to vote your way. One part of politics involves electing government leaders. The political activities leading up to an election are called a "campaign." In a political campaign, the people who are trying to get elected try to persuade voters to vote for them through speeches, advertisements, debates, and so forth.

Governments are an important part of God's design for the world. God wants all rulers to obey him and for citizens to obey the government's laws. That is why voters should think carefully and pray often about whom to vote for. We want to pick the best rulers—the ones who will do the best job.

KEY VERSE: *Now look around among yourselves, brothers, and select seven men who are well respected and are full of the Holy Spirit and wisdom. We will put them in charge of this business. (Acts 6:3)*

RELATED VERSES: *1 Kings 3:10-14; Esther 4:14; 7:1-10; Proverbs 29:2; Matthew 27:15-26; Acts 12:1-3*

Q: WHY CAN'T CHILDREN VOTE?

33

A: Young children are not allowed to vote because they have not had enough experience and education to have earned the right to vote. Also, they are not involved enough in society. In other words, they don't pay taxes, own land, drive a car, or run a business. In a sense, a person earns the right to vote by growing up.

The best way to become a good voter is to love and obey God with all your heart. If you know what God wants for your country, you will make better voting decisions than if you didn't know what God wants. Until then, you can pray for your leaders and voters, asking God to give them wisdom.

KEY VERSE: *Don't let anyone think less of you because you are young. Be an example to all believers in what you teach, in the way you live, in your love, your faith, and your purity. (1 Timothy 4:12)*

RELATED VERSES: *Exodus 20:12; 1 Kings 12:8-9; Proverbs 3:5-8; 1 Timothy 2:2*

RELATED QUESTION: *When people vote for who they want to be their leader, what if they don't want any of them?*

Q: WHAT IS DEMOCRACY?

34

A: Democracy is a type of government in which the citizens of a country elect the men and women who will lead them. These elected leaders are called representatives because they represent the people of that country—they speak for the citizens. In the election for each office (such as governor, mayor, senator, or council person), the person who gets the most votes wins the election and holds that office until the next election. In every election, the citizens can elect new leaders if they want to. Wise citizens choose their leaders very carefully, because a leader's character will determine whether he or she is a just ruler.

Be sure to pray for your country's leaders. They need God's wisdom all the time.

KEY VERSES: *When he sits on the throne as king, he must copy these laws on a scroll for himself in the presence of the Levitical priests. He must always keep this copy of the law with him and read it daily as long as he lives. That way he will learn to fear the Lord his God by obeying all the terms of this law. This regular reading will prevent him from becoming proud and acting as if he is above his fellow citizens. It will also prevent him from turning away from these commands in the smallest way. This will ensure that he and his descendants will reign for many generations in Israel. (Deuteronomy 17:18-20)*

RELATED VERSES: *Psalm 72:15; Proverbs 29:4; 1 Timothy 2:2*

NOTE TO PARENTS: *In our society, most heroes are musicians, actors, and sports figures. It is good to help our children expand their list of heroes to include leaders with exceptional character. Thinking about leaders this way helps prepare children for voting and being leaders.*

Q: WHAT IS COMMUNISM?

35

A: Communism is a system in which people own property together. No one has his or her own land, business, or house; everyone owns everything together.

In governments that have been built on this idea, the state, or government, is said to own everything. The people have very little power or freedom because everything belongs to the state. The national leaders run everything and control the elections (if elections are held).

Communism is supposed to be a big group of people who govern themselves, but communist countries usually become dictatorships of the state. National leaders do whatever they want. The people themselves become servants of the leaders and have few rights or freedoms.

KEY VERSE: *When you want a certain piece of land, you find a way to seize it. When you want someone's house, you take it by fraud and violence. No one's family or inheritance is safe with you around! (Micah 2:2)*

RELATED VERSES: *Genesis 47:18-21; Acts 2:44*

RELATED QUESTIONS: *How come communism didn't like Christians and sent them to jail or to faraway places? What is the cause of communism falling?*

NOTE TO PARENTS: *Although some government systems are better than others, all have flaws. Only God's kingdom is perfect. Only God can rule perfectly because only God is completely unselfish, loves everyone, and always knows what is best.*

Q: WHY DO GOVERNMENTS DO WRONG THINGS?

36

A: Governments do wrong things for the same reason that individual persons do wrong things—sin. Every person is sinful. That means that people are naturally self-centered, and they try to live their lives without God. Some people are more sinful than others. That is, they work very hard to cheat, lie, and steal. Governments are made up of people, so they will sometimes do wrong things unless someone is keeping an eye on them and stops them. That is why many governments are organized with a system of "checks and balances," which lets one branch of government stop the actions of another. Democratic governments hold elections every few years. That gives the people the chance to get rid of bad leaders.

The good news is that God does not ignore the deeds of leaders. He watches over those who hold authority in government. Pray that God will make your country's leaders just and wise.

KEY VERSES: *I also noticed that throughout the world there is evil in the courtroom. Yes, even the courts of law are corrupt! I said to myself, "In due season God will judge everyone, both good and bad, for all their deeds."* (Ecclesiastes 3:16-17)

RELATED VERSES: *1 Kings 2:1-3; Psalms 53:3; 94:20-23; Romans 3:10; 1 Timothy 2:2*

Q: WHY DO GOVERNMENTS DO THINGS WRONG?

37

A: Governments don't always do things wrong, even though people sometimes like to complain about the government. Government forms and programs can often be very complicated, and that's frustrating for a lot of people who have to deal with them. Of course, government leaders and officials will sometimes make mistakes and blunders. We all make mistakes. No government is perfect because no human being is perfect.

Although no government is perfect, people need government. If we didn't have leaders, laws, police officers, firefighters, tax collectors, and other government workers, every person would do whatever he or she wanted, and the country would be in a mess.

KEY VERSE: *Remind your people to submit to the government and its officers. They should be obedient, always ready to do what is good. (Titus 3:1)*

RELATED VERSE: *1 Timothy 2:2*

ENVIRONMENTAL CONCERNS

Q: HOW MUCH DOES RECYCLING HELP?

38

A: It helps a lot. Recycling is important because people are using the natural resources of the earth very rapidly. For example, crude oil is used to heat homes and to make gasoline for cars and trucks. Many other products also come from oil, including plastics, tires, and jet fuel. Yet there is only so much oil in the earth. When it is used up, it will all be gone.

Recycling used oil, plastic, and rubber makes these resources stretch. We don't use up things so fast. And we are able to reuse the materials to make other things. God does not want us to be wasteful.

At the same time, we don't need to fear running out of the things we need. God created us. He created this earth. He put us on this earth to live and enjoy it. He provides the things we need. If we run out of oil, it will be OK, because God will still be in charge, and he will always provide the things we need.

So recycle and don't be wasteful, but don't be afraid of running out of things either. Just be a responsible user of the good things God lets you have and use.

KEY VERSE: *"Now gather the leftovers," Jesus told his disciples, "so that nothing is wasted." (John 6:12)*

RELATED VERSE: *Proverbs 12:27*

RELATED QUESTIONS: *Why do we have to drop things off at a recycling depot? How much garbage can recycling plants hold? What do they do with the garbage?*

NOTE TO PARENTS: *You may want to mention that garbage goes to landfills. Pretty soon all the landfills will be filled up with trash and garbage. Often the garbage pollutes our soil and water. We've used more nonrenewable resources since World War II than we used in all of history before. Recycling is simply a responsible way to live.*

Q: HOW CAN THEY RECYCLE MILK JUGS AFTER PEOPLE STEP ON THEM?

SNOWSHOES
FOR SALE
75¢ A PAIR

MILK
MILK

MILK

39

A: When items such as plastic milk jugs are recycled, they are combined with other plastic items, melted, and used to make other products. For example, recycled plastic bottles are often used to make playground equipment. Other kinds of bottles and containers are reused this way too. The bottles are *never* just washed out and refilled with milk. The government does not permit that because it would spread germs and disease. So stepping on empty milk jugs doesn't hurt in recycling.

KEY VERSES: *People know how to mine silver and refine gold. They know how to dig iron from the earth and smelt copper from stone. (Job 28:1-2)*

RELATED VERSE: *John 6:12*

RELATED QUESTIONS: *How do you recycle cans? When people recycle newspapers, how do they get the ink off?*

Q: WHY DO PEOPLE LITTER SO MUCH WHEN THEY CAN JUST THROW THEIR TRASH IN THE GARBAGE CAN?

40

A: Some people litter by accident. They are careless or do not pay attention to what happens to their food wrappers and other trash. People who litter on purpose, however, do so because they are not showing respect for other people or the earth.

We should pick up trash instead of littering or ignoring the litter on the ground. Just because we didn't drop it doesn't mean we should say, "It's not my mess." We are all keepers of God's earth. If everyone pitched in and picked up a little, the world would be a nicer, tidier place.

KEY VERSE: *The Lord God placed the man in the Garden of Eden to tend and care for it. (Genesis 2:15)*

RELATED VERSES: *Proverbs 18:9; 26:13; Romans 8:19-22*

RELATED QUESTIONS: *Why do people litter? If littering is against the law, just how important is this law?*

NOTE TO PARENTS: *Kids often object by saying, "But I didn't make the mess!" without realizing that their objection is irrelevant. We all live in a community, and we all share in the care of the environment. God's way is for us to look out for each other. Take your kids out with bags and gloves and clean up the litter at the school or the park and use the opportunity to teach these principles.*

Q: WHY DO PEOPLE WANT TO WRECK THE EARTH WITH POLLUTION?

41

A: Most people don't want to wreck the earth. Instead, people pollute because they don't think about the consequences of polluting or because they don't care about the damage it might do. Some may actually believe that littering and dumping waste really don't matter, that they don't hurt anything, or that it's someone else's job to clean it up.

Some people pollute because they are just too lazy to walk to a trash can. They are more concerned with doing things the easy way than with doing what is right.

KEY VERSE: *For we know that all creation has been groaning as in the pains of childbirth right up to the present time. (Romans 8:22)*

RELATED VERSES: *Proverbs 6:6-11; 20:4; Romans 8:19-21*

RELATED QUESTIONS: *Why do people pollute the world all the time? When they flatten the cars, does it pollute the air? Why are we ruining the earth if we only have one?*

NOTE TO PARENTS: *Whenever you answer a child's question about what others do wrong, be careful to guard against judging others. Help your child to focus on his or her own behavior and not judge others. God loves everyone, and we don't know why people do what they do. Pray together for the people you see doing wrong, that God will bless them with wisdom and truth.*

42

A: The main reason there is so much pollution in the cities is that there are so many people. Lots of people means lots of cars, buses, trucks, restaurants, stores, industry, and garbage. In most cities with all the buildings and traffic, it can be difficult to clean up right away. Sometimes events in cities (such as parades, games, concerts, and rallies) attract lots of people who litter. If one person in a field throws a wrapper on the ground, it may not seem like a big deal. But if 100,000 people in the city each throw a wrapper on the ground, that's 100,000 wrappers!

All the traffic and factories add to air pollution and noise pollution, too. In smaller towns and out in the country, there aren't as many cars, trucks, buses, and people to contribute to the pollution problems.

KEY VERSE: *Upright citizens bless a city and make it prosper, but the talk of the wicked tears it apart. (Proverbs 11:11)*

RELATED VERSES: *Genesis 2:15; Proverbs 11:10; 14:4*

RELATED QUESTIONS: *If smog hurts people, why do people make smog out of factories? How do cars make so much smoke? Why do people live in this trash? Is there some kind of filter you can put on the smog? How does pollution kill us?*

Q: WHY DO SOME COMPANIES THROW DANGEROUS CHEMICALS INTO RIVERS AND OCEANS?

43

A: It used to be that companies dumped a lot of chemicals into rivers and oceans because they didn't know that the chemicals were hurting anything. But when it was discovered how harmful some chemicals can be, the government made laws against dumping them. Now if companies pollute, they are disobeying the law. Sadly, some companies continue to dump dangerous chemicals into our waterways, even though they know they should dispose of them in safer ways. They do this because it's expensive to be careful and clean, and they don't want to spend the money.

KEY VERSE: *Those who love money will never have enough. How absurd to think that wealth brings true happiness! (Ecclesiastes 5:10)*

RELATED QUESTIONS: *Why do people throw chemicals into the water? When water gets dirty, how do they get it clean? Why would people want to kill fish just for a place to dump their waste? If people know chemicals are bad, why don't they dump them in space?*

NOTE TO PARENTS: *It is easy to pollute by disposing of chemicals improperly, because disposing of them properly can be time consuming and expensive. This is why many consumers routinely throw away oil, paint, and other chemicals in unsafe ways. Do your best to set a good example and dispose of these things as safely as possible, even if it is difficult or costs you money.*

Q: WHY DO PEOPLE LIVE ALL THEIR LIVES IN A CITY AND ONLY GO OUT INTO THE COUNTRYSIDE FOR PICNICS?

BATTERIES

SNAKES &
LADDERS

CHECKERS

44

A: Most people live in cities because that's where their jobs are. People need jobs to make money so they can buy food, clothes, and everything else they need. And they know it's very convenient to live close to their job. So they live near their place of work. Many people also like the busyness and the many activities to choose from in the city.

The countryside is a nice change of pace. It is a lot calmer and more peaceful than the city, and there is much less pollution there. So people like to go there occasionally for vacations and picnics. It's a nice relaxing break from their normal routine.

KEY VERSE: *That night some shepherds were in the fields outside the village, guarding their flocks of sheep. (Luke 2:8)*

RELATED VERSES: *Psalm 19:1; Amos 9:14*

RELATED QUESTIONS: *How can people live that way? Why is it called Mother Nature instead of Father Nature? Where did the phrase "Mother Nature" come from?*

45

**A:** People cut down trees

1. to make paper
2. to get wood for building houses, furniture, and other things
3. to clear land for new houses and buildings
4. to clear land for farms

It is all right to cut down trees because new trees can be planted in their place. We need paper for newspapers, magazines, and books, and paper is recyclable. We need wood for building. We need houses to live in. We need farmland to grow food.

This doesn't mean that people should cut down trees anywhere and anytime they feel like it. And they certainly shouldn't cut down trees just to be destructive. Trees provide beauty, shade, and places for birds to nest. Some trees provide flowers and fruit. And some trees help stop the wind; others help prevent soil erosion. We should take care of the trees we have.

KEY VERSE: *Joshua replied, "If the hill country of Ephraim is not large enough for you, clear out land for yourselves in the forest where the Perizzites and Rephaites live."* *(Joshua 17:15)*

RELATED VERSES: *Genesis 6:14; 22:3; Exodus 37:1; 1 Kings 5:1-10*

RELATED QUESTIONS: *If there are lots of trees in the world, why don't people set aside certain trees to be cut down? Why do the woodcutters destroy God's world?*

Q: WHAT CAN CHILDREN DO TO HELP TAKE BETTER CARE OF THE WORLD?

46

A: Sometimes it seems as though children can't do very much to make a difference in the world. After all, adults own the factories, stores, and restaurants and drive the trucks, buses, and cars. But children can help a lot. Here are a few ideas to get you started:

1. Do not litter; throw your trash away instead of throwing it on the ground.
2. Recycle paper, plastic, glass, oil, and anything else that can be recycled.
3. Take good care of your pets; they are part of God's world too.
4. Don't waste food; take only as much as you can eat.
5. Don't waste water; turn off the faucet when you're done using it.
6. Don't waste electricity; turn off the lights when you don't need them.
7. Live simply; be content with things that are a little less expensive or fancy instead of insisting on new toys or clothes.

KEY VERSE: *You put us in charge of everything you made, giving us authority over all things. (Psalm 8:6)*

RELATED VERSES: *Genesis 1:28-31; Proverbs 12:10; 24:30-34; John 6:12*

RELATED QUESTIONS: *Why doesn't everybody participate in making a better place to live? Why don't people try to save our world? Why are we waiting to take better care of our world?*

ANIMALS

47

A: The biggest reason some animals are becoming extinct is disruption of habitat. People move in and take away the land used by the animals. Some people don't seem to care what happens to the plants and animals of the earth. They just do whatever they want, regardless of the consequences to nature. But God has given human beings the job of taking care of the world. That means taking good care of *all* of it, animals included.

Remember that this all starts with you. Take good care of your pets, don't litter so they have a clean place to live, and take good care of God's earth. After all, it all belongs to God, and we are his stewards.

KEY VERSE: *For all the animals of the forest are mine, and I own the cattle on a thousand hills. (Psalm 50:10)*

RELATED VERSES: *Genesis 1:28-31; Proverbs 12:10; Ezekiel 34:25*

RELATED QUESTIONS: *Should we stop killing animals? Should we pray for endangered animals?*

48

A: When sin entered the world, all of creation was damaged. Ever since that time, pain and suffering have been a part of life. People and animals suffer—no one escapes.

Probably the greatest danger to animals is other animals that attack and kill them for food. Animals eat each other because they are part of the food chain. They need the food to survive. Some animals eat only plants, but many eat other animals. For example, dragonflies eat mosquitoes, birds eat worms and other insects, cats eat mice and birds, and some big fish eat baby ducks. Some animals, called scavengers, eat dead animals that they find in the woods or along the highway. God created animals that way. If all the animals continued to live, soon the world would be filled with them.

KEY VERSES: *You send the darkness, and it becomes night, when all the forest animals prowl about. Then the young lions roar for their food, but they are dependent on God. (Psalm 104:20-21)*

RELATED VERSES: *Genesis 3:14-19; Job 39:13-18, 26-30; Ecclesiastes 10:8-9; Isaiah 11:6; Matthew 10:29*

Q: WHY DO PEOPLE KILL ANIMALS TO EAT WHEN THEY COULD JUST BUY FOOD AT THE STORE?

49

A: Many years ago, everyone had to hunt for food. They would gather plants and kill animals. Then some people began to raise fruits and vegetables and sell them. Others raised animals and sold them. Eventually, there were grocery stores where people could buy the fruit, vegetables, milk, and meat they needed to eat. But for meat to be available at a store, someone has to kill the animals.

It certainly is more convenient to buy meat at a store than to raise chickens or hunt wild pigs. But some people enjoy hunting, so they hunt deer, moose, pheasant, or some other animal instead of buying all their meat at the store.

No matter where we get our food, we should always thank God for it. The food we have is part of what God provides for us so we can live.

KEY VERSES: *God blessed Noah and his sons and told them, "Multiply and fill the earth. All the wild animals, large and small, and all the birds and fish will be afraid of you. I have placed them in your power. I have given them to you for food, just as I have given you grain and vegetables." (Genesis 9:1-3)*

RELATED VERSES: *Acts 10:9-13; 1 Corinthians 10:30-31*

RELATED QUESTIONS: *Why do people think we shouldn't eat animals or meat? Why do people think we shouldn't eat animals even if they're raised for it?*

50

A: Some people who don't care about animals are mean to them for fun. Other people hurt animals without meaning to when they are angry or frustrated. For example, someone might be having a very bad day. Then, when this person comes home and the pet has done something annoying, the person takes out his or her anger on the pet. We don't always know why other people are mean, but we can ask God to help us be kind and not mean. He can help us take good care of his creation.

KEY VERSE: *The godly are concerned for the welfare of their animals, but even the kindness of the wicked is cruel. (Proverbs 12:10)*

RELATED VERSES: *Proverbs 16:32; Colossians 3:12*

RELATED QUESTIONS: *Why do people sometimes try to hurt harmless animals? Why are people mean to God's creatures? Why do we kill animals even though they do no harm?*

Q: DO ANIMALS HAVE FEELINGS JUST LIKE PEOPLE DO?

51

A: Animals have feelings, but they are not exactly like people. Think about your body. Animals have bodies just as we have bodies, but they're not the same kind of bodies. Humans have a unique brain structure. They can think about the future. A dog will bury a bone, but she won't sit on the porch and wonder if she has buried enough bones for retirement. It is a lot like that with feelings. A dog can feel lonely, sad, afraid, and hungry. But the dog cannot think about the reasons for those feelings. The dog only responds to certain conditions (for example, he feels alone and sad in a kennel or afraid when the thunder roars and the lightning cracks). God has given us more complex emotions that we can experience, enjoy, use, and direct.

KEY VERSE: *Do you think we are cattle? Do you think we have no intelligence? (Job 18:3)*

RELATED VERSE: *Proverbs 26:11*

RELATED QUESTIONS: *Do animals have feelings like we do? Why can't animals have feelings?*

52

A: Every good thing that we enjoy is a gift from God. Many people often enjoy their pets and like having them around. They grow very attached to a favorite pet. Animals are loyal, they appreciate their masters, and after they are trained, they don't give their masters much grief. Many people come to like their pets very much. Some people treat their pets as though they are members of the family. So when a pet gets lost or dies, the master feels very sad and may even cry. It is OK to cry when you lose a pet that you loved.

KEY VERSES: *If you had one hundred sheep, and one of them strayed away and was lost in the wilderness, wouldn't you leave the ninety-nine others to go and search for the lost one until you found it? And then you would joyfully carry it home on your shoulders. When you arrived, you would call together your friends and neighbors to rejoice with you because your lost sheep was found. (Luke 15:4-6)*

RELATED VERSE: *1 Timothy 6:17*

RELATED QUESTION: *Why shouldn't people cry when their pet dies? The pet is sort of like family.*

Q: WHY DO SOME ANIMALS LOOK FUNNY?

53

A: God is very creative. He made a huge variety of plants and animals—hundreds of thousands of kinds. And remember that *every person* is special and different. This variety is part of God's creative genius. It is part of the beauty he built into the world.

Some animals look funny because they are built a certain way to help them live in their environment and to get food. An armadillo, for example, has a hard shell that protects it from other animals. A lizard has a long, sticky tongue to help it catch flies to eat. An anteater has a long nose to help it eat ants. The giraffe's long neck helps it eat leaves from tall trees. God made all animals with amazing mechanisms for survival, and that's just one of the wonders of God himself.

KEY VERSES: *Take a look at the mighty hippopotamus. I made it, just as I made you. It eats grass like an ox. See its powerful loins and the muscles of its belly. Its tail is as straight as a cedar. The sinews of its thighs are tightly knit together. Its bones are tubes of bronze. Its limbs are bars of iron. It is a prime example of God's amazing handiwork. Only its Creator can threaten it. (Job 40:15-19)*

RELATED VERSES: *Genesis 1:20-25; Psalm 19:1*

RELATED QUESTION: *Why were animals made?*

NOTE TO PARENTS: *Encourage your children with the fact that God created them to be wonderfully unique.*

Q: WHY DO CATS AND DOGS FIGHT?

54

A: Usually cats and dogs fight because they are trying to protect their territory. It is natural for animals to compete for dominance (to see who is the strongest). Dogs and cats that are raised with each other usually don't fight. They are used to each other and get along pretty well.

KEY VERSES: *In that day the wolf and the lamb will live together; the leopard and the goat will be at peace. Calves and yearlings will be safe among lions, and a little child will lead them all. The cattle will graze among bears. Cubs and calves will lie down together. And lions will eat grass as the livestock do. (Isaiah 11:6-7)*

RELATED QUESTIONS: *Why do animals fight each other? Why do cats chase after rats? Why do dogs chase cats? Why does my cat chase and fight my neighbor's big fat cat? How come guinea pigs fight other guinea pigs? How come crabs fight other crabs? How come fighting fish fight with other fighting fish?*

THE
ENTERTAINMENT
INDUSTRY

Q: WHY DO MOVIES HAVE WEIRDOS FOR STARS?

55

A: Not all movie stars are weirdos. Many are normal people who live pretty normal lives. The news media don't report these normal lives. They report the abnormal ones—the weird cases. So we hear a lot about the weirdos and nothing about the rest of the normal stars. That makes it seem as though all of the movie and television actors are weird, but they're not.

Some stars act weird on purpose in order to get attention. In other words, they put on an act so newspaper and magazine stories will be written about them. They think this will help their career.

Others act weird because they have an exaggerated idea of their own importance. Because so many people tell them how great they are and because they get a lot of attention and money for doing their job, they sometimes think they can do anything they want. So they take drugs, trash hotel rooms, marry and divorce several times, and do other shocking things. The sin of pride can make people do strange things.

KEY VERSES: *Everything they do is for show. . . . They enjoy the attention they get on the streets. (Matthew 23:5, 7)*

RELATED VERSES: *Psalm 49:16-18; Proverbs 11:2; 12:23; 16:8, 27; Matthew 23:5-12; Luke 6:24-26*

RELATED QUESTION: *Why does Hollywood make movies?*

NOTE TO PARENTS: *Children often idolize movie stars and athletes for the wrong reasons. Help your children understand the difference between liking a person's skills and wanting to be like that person. We should strive to be like people who are wise and good, not like those who are popular.*

Q: WHY DO PEOPLE PUT GARBAGE IN THEIR HEADS BY WATCHING BAD MOVIES?

56

A: Junk entertainment is like junk food—it tastes good even though it's bad for us. Many people watch garbage on TV and in the movies because they like it, even though it is bad for them.

God wants us to be *discerning*. He wants us to recognize junk entertainment for what it is and avoid it, even if it seems fun or harmless. Ratings help many people decide whether or not to see certain movies or TV shows. A movie rated G is said to be all right for "General Audiences." In other words, people of all ages will probably not be offended or hurt by anything in the movie.

The ratings are not always right, however. That's why it is helpful to read reviews or talk with others about a movie or TV show. Some movies can have a mild rating (for example, G or PG) and yet teach some pretty bad stuff about God and life.

Be careful about what you watch because once you've watched something, you can't unwatch it.

KEY VERSE: *Fix your thoughts on what is true and honorable and right. Think about things that are pure and lovely and admirable. Think about things that are excellent and worthy of praise. (Philippians 4:8)*

RELATED VERSES: *Deuteronomy 7:26; Psalms 101:3; 106:35-36; James 1:5-8*

RELATED QUESTIONS: *How come parents don't want us to watch bad shows and movies? If some movies are so bad, why are they fun to watch?*

NOTE TO PARENTS: *What you model is what your children will become. Choose entertainment wisely; think critically about the shows and movies you consider watching.*

Q: WHY IS THERE SO MUCH FIGHTING ON TV?

57

A: One reason is that there is so much fighting in real life. Some people have not learned to control their temper, so there is a lot of fighting. God wants us to overlook insults and stay calm when people try to make us mad. Too many people think they have no choice but to blow their top.

Another reason TV has a lot of fighting is that many people like to see other people fight. A lot of people watch shows with fighting in them, so the studios produce them and the networks show them. The TV and studio bosses often say they show fighting because it is an important part of the story and they have to be realistic. That may be true, but the real reason is money.

KEY VERSE: *Good people enjoy the positive results of their words, but those who are treacherous crave violence. (Proverbs 13:2)*

RELATED VERSES: *Genesis 6:5-6; Proverbs 20:3; 26:21*

RELATED QUESTIONS: *How can people make movies and shows about fighting and hurting and shooting each other? Why do we enjoy seeing other people get hurt?*

Q: HOW COME PEOPLE PUT BAD MOVIES ON TV?

58

A: Because lots of people watch them. The moviemakers and the network bosses try to make as much money as possible. If a lot of people watch a certain movie, the television network can make a lot of money through advertising. The networks know that lots of people watch bad shows. Instead of watching bad movies, we should ignore them by changing channels or turning off the TV set. If a lot of people wrote the TV stations and complained about the bad movies, maybe the networks wouldn't show them anymore.

Remember that bad is bad no matter how many people do it. You don't have to watch bad movies just because they're popular.

KEY VERSES: *Stop loving this evil world and all that it offers you, for when you love the world, you show that you do not have the love of the Father in you. For the world offers only the lust for physical pleasure, the lust for everything we see, and pride in our possessions. These are not from the Father. They are from this evil world. (1 John 2:15-16)*

RELATED VERSES: *Psalm 101:3; Philippians 4:8*

RELATED QUESTIONS: *What in the world is a V chip? Who invented the V chip? Why do the fighting video games make people want to fight?*

NOTE TO PARENTS: *Telling children they can't watch something "because it's bad" will arouse their curiosity and often backfire. Instead, tell your children what's in the show and why it's bad, or how it will adversely affect them. This will allow them to share in the decision, or at least to see that you have good reasons for it.*

Q: WHY DO MOVIE COMPANIES MAKE SCARY MOVIES IF THEY KNOW PEOPLE WILL HAVE NIGHTMARES?

59

A: Many people want to see scary movies and will pay money to see them. The companies that make these movies don't care about whether or not they are scary or bad. They just want to make money.

God doesn't want us to be afraid of monsters, demons, ghosts, and prowlers. He wants us to think good thoughts and be confident in his care for us, because he loves us and created us to enjoy life. So if something you're watching scares you, stop watching it. And if you see something that bothers you, talk to your parents about it and pray together that God will protect you and give you good dreams. God does not want you to have nightmares.

KEY VERSE: *I will lie down in peace and sleep, for you alone, O Lord, will keep me safe. (Psalm 4:8)*

RELATED VERSES: *Psalm 101:3; Romans 8:38-39*

RELATED QUESTIONS: *Why do people scare others with scary movies? Why does God let Satan scare us with scary movies? Why isn't there just a certain channel for horror shows? Why do they put kids in horror movies, then rate them R? Why do people make bad movies? Why do people make movies if they put fighting and violence in them?*

Q: WHY ARE SOME THINGS ON VIDEOS FUNNY FOR ADULTS BUT NOT FOR KIDS?

60

A: Some jokes are funny for adults but not for children because kids and adults have different kinds of humor. Each group finds different things funny. Also, adults have experiences that kids haven't had. They laugh at things that they know about. For example, a joke about working on the job, paying income tax, or raising children wouldn't be very funny to children. Only people who know about those situations would get the joke.

A good family movie will often include humor for the kids and for the adults so the whole family can enjoy it together.

KEY VERSE: *It's like this: When I was a child, I spoke and thought and reasoned as a child does. But when I grew up, I put away childish things. (1 Corinthians 13:11)*

RELATED QUESTION: *Why do people laugh at jokes that aren't funny?*

NOTE TO PARENTS: *Humor and laughter are gifts from God. If your children have a great sense of humor and can readily make others laugh, encourage them to use the gift wisely and not to abuse it with cruelty or offensive language.*

Q: WHY WON'T PARENTS LET KIDS WATCH CERTAIN SHOWS THE KIDS WANT TO WATCH?

61

A: Because God gives parents the responsibility to guide their children, and sometimes parents know something about a show that the kids don't know. Parents know that the show will have violence or swearing or will make bad things look good. They may not let their children watch those kinds of shows. Most parents also know that too much TV is not good. Good parents put limits on how much television and what shows their family can watch.

KEY VERSE: *Children, obey your parents because you belong to the Lord, for this is the right thing to do. (Ephesians 6:1)*

RELATED VERSES: *Psalm 101:3; Proverbs 4:23*

RELATED QUESTIONS: *If you get cable and there's a channel with all bad shows, why don't your parents phone and ask the cable company to take that off their bill? Why do people make bad shows in the first place? Why do people like TV with so many channels?*

Q: WHY DO PEOPLE LIKE DIFFERENT KINDS OF MUSIC?

62

A: People like various kinds of music because people have different tastes. Each person is unique and special—a part of the variety in God's creation. It's the same with people's tastes in food. Everyone has favorite foods. We wouldn't expect everyone to eat and like all the same foods.

Certain groups of people like certain kinds of music. People of one nationality may like one kind, and people from one area of the country may have their own musical likes and dislikes. Some people just listen to whatever is popular.

We should choose music (and other forms of entertainment) wisely, because it's something we put into our mind. God wants us to think about good things.

KEY VERSE: *Just as the mouth tastes good food, the ear tests the words it hears. (Job 34:3)*

RELATED VERSES: *Judges 5:3; Psalm 81:1-3; Proverbs 4:23; Ephesians 5:19*

RELATED QUESTIONS: *Why does God let you rot your brain with bad music? Why does God let people sing bad music? Who invented music? How come music gets so loud? How many types of music are there? How many songs are there in the world? How can people listen to rock music?*

Q: WHY ARE MUSICIANS TREATED LIKE IDOLS?

63

A: Everybody looks up to somebody. God made us this way so we could learn and grow into people who love and obey him. He gives us parents to start the process, and as we get older we choose others from whom to learn.

Many people choose to idolize musicians because they appear in the spotlight a lot. They are featured in newspapers and magazines and on TV and are held up as heroes. Many people look up to them simply because of all the attention they get.

Others "worship" musicians because their music makes them feel something very deeply. That is the way art works—it touches people's emotions.

And others idolize musicians because they assume that being rich and famous is important. Not all musicians are rich and famous, but those who are may appear to be especially successful or great.

KEY VERSE: *Friends, why are you doing this? We are merely human beings like yourselves! We have come to bring you the Good News that you should turn from these worthless things to the living God, who made heaven and earth, the sea, and everything in them. (Acts 14:15)*

RELATED VERSES: *Acts 14:11-18*

NOTE TO PARENTS: *We should choose our heroes carefully, and we should be careful not to idolize them. Encourage your children to look up to those who love God and try to do what is right. Help them to realize that no one is perfect, not even great heroes.*

Q: WHY ARE THERE COMMERCIALS ALL THE TIME WHEN GOOD SHOWS ARE ON TV?

64

A: The commercials pay for the shows. That is, the companies that show the programs get paid by the companies that make the commercials. If the networks did not show the commercials, they would have no money to pay for the programs. A lot of people watch the very popular shows, so that is why you see so many commercials. The companies advertising want to show their commercials when a lot of people are watching.

KEY VERSE: *Do not cheat or rob anyone. Always pay your hired workers promptly. (Leviticus 19:13)*

RELATED VERSE: *Proverbs 11:26*

RELATED QUESTIONS: *Why are there commercials? Why are there commercials on TV and not in movies? Why do they show previews of movies? Why not just make it a surprise?*

Q: WHEN YOU WANT TO HAVE SOMETHING YOU SEE ON A TV COMMERCIAL, WHY DOESN'T YOUR MOM LET YOU HAVE IT?

65

A: Many times the products advertised on television look much better than they really are, and your parents know it. Your parents have the responsibility to guide and protect you. Their job is to teach you God's ways and God's wisdom. They may not let you have something that looks exciting on TV because they know that it isn't going to be as great as the commercial shows. Or they may know that you do not need it or that it costs too much money. Or they know that it would actually be bad for you, even if you can't imagine how.

KEY VERSE: *Then he said, "Beware! Don't be greedy for what you don't have. Real life is not measured by how much we own." (Luke 12:15)*

RELATED VERSES: *Ephesians 6:1-3; 1 John 2:15-17*

RELATED QUESTIONS: *When you get something you saw on a commercial, why don't you like it? Why do commercials have to say, "It's not available at stores"?*

FAMILY MATTERS

66

A: God's plan is for a husband and wife to stay together and not get divorced. But all people have weaknesses. No one is perfect. That is why troubles arise in all relationships, even between two people who love each other very much.

When a man and a woman get married, they promise to stay with each other for life. They know it won't always be easy, but they want to work out their problems and stay together. When the arguments and other conflicts and pressures come, some people don't know how to handle them, and their problems get worse. Usually the problems start small and then grow. Eventually, these problems can become so big that the husband or the wife or both just give up and decide to end their marriage. Some don't try that hard; they divorce because they choose not to work out their problems.

But God wants Christians to stay married and work things out. He knows that when they do, their lives will be better for it.

KEY VERSES: *Jesus replied, "Moses permitted divorce as a concession to your hard-hearted wickedness, but it was not what God had originally intended. And I tell you this, a man who divorces his wife and marries another commits adultery—unless his wife has been unfaithful."* *(Matthew 19:8-9)*

RELATED VERSES: *Proverbs 18:22; Matthew 19:3-12; Romans 3:23; 1 Corinthians 7:10-11, 26-28*

RELATED QUESTIONS: *Why do people marry if they're just going to get divorced? Why do some people just get married without having a ceremony? What is the youngest kids can get married?*

Q: WHY DO SOME BROTHERS AND SISTERS FIGHT?

67

A: Most fights between brothers and sisters are normal. When you live with somebody, sometimes you get annoyed with each other, or you both try to use the same thing, or you both want to occupy the same space, or you each want to do things differently. This happens in every family—even in families where people love each other very much.

The next time you disagree with your brother or sister, here's what to do. Try to state your differences without yelling or hitting. If you are upset, calm down and lower your voice. Tell the person how you feel. It also helps to try to see things from the other person's point of view. Listen to each other without interrupting. Then as you talk it out, you can suggest a way to solve the problem. Maybe you can take turns. Maybe you can give up a little of what you wanted. Remember that you're both on the same team.

Every conflict is an opportunity for you to learn one of life's most valuable skills—how to get along with others. It will not happen by magic. You have to learn how to do it, like learning how to ride a bike. It takes work, prayer, and practice.

KEY VERSES: *Never pay back evil for evil to anyone. Do things in such a way that everyone can see you are honorable. Do your part to live in peace with everyone, as much as possible. (Romans 12:17-18)*

RELATED VERSES: *Proverbs 15:1; 17:9, 13, 27; 20:22; 26:21; Romans 12:10; Ephesians 4:32; 1 John 3:11-12*

RELATED QUESTIONS: *Brothers and sisters are supposed to be nice to each other, but how come they always fight? Why don't brothers and sisters get along? Why can't sisters be more supportive?*

Q: WHY DO SOME KIDS HAVE STEPMOTHERS OR STEPFATHERS?

STEP DAD   ROPE DAD

68

A: Stepmothers and stepfathers come into the picture whenever a parent remarries. That is, one of the parents dies or divorces the other. If the other parent gets married again, the children get a new mother or father. This person is called a *stepmother* or *stepfather*.

For example, suppose a boy's mother and father get divorced and the boy lives with his mother. If the mother remarries, her new husband becomes the boy's stepfather. Or suppose a girl's mother dies. If the girl's father remarries, his new wife becomes the girl's stepmother. If the stepfather or stepmother brings children into the family, the children of the two families become stepbrothers and stepsisters. And if the newly married parents have more children after they get married, those children become half brothers and half sisters of the children that came before them.

Divorce and remarriage can be confusing. But remember that no matter what label we give to the parents and kids in a family, they are still all part of one family. It doesn't matter how they came together.

KEY VERSE: *A wife is married to her husband as long as he lives. If her husband dies, she is free to marry whomever she wishes, but this must be a marriage acceptable to the Lord. (1 Corinthians 7:39)*

RELATED VERSES: *Matthew 19:3-12; 1 Corinthians 7:1-40*

RELATED QUESTIONS: *What are half brothers and half sisters? Why do parents sometimes not like their children?*

Q: WHY DID PEOPLE USE TO HAVE SO MANY KIDS?

69

A: One reason parents used to have more kids is that before modern medicine, more children died young, from disease and other problems, than die today. Parents could not be sure that their children would live. Another reason families of the past had a lot of children is that they needed many family members to help with the family work—around the house or on the farm. Modern medicine has also made it easier than ever to prevent pregnancy.

God loves families of all shapes and sizes. Today, some families do have a lot of children. But it is not as common as it used to be.

KEY VERSE: *God blessed them and told them, "Multiply and fill the earth and subdue it. Be masters over the fish and birds and all the animals." (Genesis 1:28)*

RELATED VERSES: *Genesis 17:6; 42:32; Psalm 127:3-5*

Q: HOW ARE FAMILIES DIFFERENT NOW FROM THE WAY THEY USED TO BE?

70

A: In some ways families are very different. Before cars and planes were invented, families were very close and lots of relatives lived together. Most families were also larger, with more children. New inventions have caused many families to spread far apart. Now people can travel long distances very quickly by car, airplane, bus, boat, or train to visit family, and they can communicate with each other on the phone and through electronic mail.

But in many ways families are still the same. Families start with a mom and a dad. The parents have parents. Kids have grandparents. And sometimes the grand-parents or other relatives live with the family.

KEY VERSES: *The church should care for any widow who has no one else to care for her. But if she has children or grandchildren, their first responsibility is to show godliness at home and repay their parents by taking care of them. This is something that pleases God very much. (1 Timothy 5:3-4)*

RELATED VERSES: *Acts 16:33-34; 1 Timothy 3:4-5; 5:8; 2 Timothy 1:5*

RELATED QUESTION: *How come families changed?*

CHANGING TECHNOLOGY

"NEW COMPUTERS" &
DAY-OLD COMPUTERS
SOLD HERE

71

A: Technology is changing very fast. Just think of some of the things that people use every day:

- Television was invented in 1926.
- Penicillin was first used to cure disease in 1929.
- The microwave oven was invented in 1947.
- The VCR was invented in 1965.
- The personal computer was invented in 1972.
- Cellular phones were first used by the public in 1979.
- The World Wide Web was created in 1990.

These recent inventions have become very important to us. And right now, as you are reading this, people are inventing new machines, medicines, appliances, computers, and other technologies that can help us even more. This all comes from the creativity God gave us.

KEY VERSE: *And people should eat and drink and enjoy the fruits of their labor, for these are gifts from God. (Ecclesiastes 3:13)*

RELATED VERSES: *Proverbs 25:2; Ecclesiastes 1:9-10; 3:1-15*

RELATED QUESTIONS: *What in technology is changing? What is technology?*

Q: HOW DID COMPUTERS GET SO SMART?

72

A: Computers do not think, so they aren't smart in the way that human beings are smart. Computers simply process information very, very fast. They receive and send electrical signals according to a set of rules, called instructions, built into the main chip. The computers of today seem "smarter" than older ones because they run much faster, and because they have more instructions built into them. But they still just process information according to a set of rules.

Some people think that human beings are very special computers, with the "main chip" in their head. But this is not true. A person is much more than just a brain, and a brain is much more than a big computer chip. A person is a combination of body, soul, and spirit. A person is created in the image of God. Computers are just machines. They aren't anything like "smart."

KEY VERSE: *For the Lord grants wisdom! From his mouth come knowledge and understanding. (Proverbs 2:6)*

RELATED VERSES: *Genesis 1:27; Psalms 8:5; 139:13-16; Jeremiah 9:23-24*

RELATED QUESTIONS: *How come people think computers will take over the world? Why do we need computers? Who invented computers?*

Q: HOW DO COMPUTERS GET VIRUSES?

73

A: A computer virus is a program that copies itself to another computer by attaching itself to programs or data. Computers get viruses when people load or run infected files on their computers. They are called viruses because they work like living viruses—by making copies of themselves and attaching themselves to, or "infecting," another machine. Most do this when someone opens or runs an infected file on their own computer.

Viruses don't just arise out of nowhere. People write them. Some of those who write viruses claim that it's not their fault if users get infected files. But that is just an example of how sin and selfishness can blind us to the truth. God says we should look out for each other, respect each other, and love each other, because everything we do affects someone else. It is true that most viruses do not cause any damage or harm. But some are written to cause mischief or damage to data. And even the harmless ones take time and energy to get rid of. Damaging someone else's property is wrong.

KEY VERSES: *Just as damaging as a mad man shooting a lethal weapon is someone who lies to a friend and then says, "I was only joking." (Proverbs 26:18-19)*

RELATED VERSES: *Proverbs 2:12-14; Luke 6:31*

Q: HOW COME THE KEYS ON THE KEYBOARD ARE NOT IN ALPHABETICAL ORDER?

74

A: Computer keyboards made today have the same layout as the very first typewriter ever made. The typewriter was invented by Christopher Sholes of Milwaukee, Wisconsin, in 1867. The layout for the keys he came up with is called a QWERTY layout because those letters are the first six letters on the top row. Sholes chose this layout because he believed it would be easy to use—the placement of the letters would make it easy to type English words quickly without jamming the parts of the typewriter. Typewriters and computer keyboards of today don't have any parts that can jam, but everyone is so used to using the QWERTY layout that we keep using it.

KEY VERSE: *Any story sounds true until someone sets the record straight. (Proverbs 18:17)*

Q: WHY DO PEOPLE SURF ON THE INTERNET?

75

People "surf" the Internet for many reasons:

- Curiosity—it can be interesting; they want to see what's there.
- Education—it can be informative; they want to answer questions or learn something.
- Information—it can tell them something they need to know, such as a weather forecast, a sports schedule, or the route to a place.
- Entertainment—it can be fun; they want to listen to music, meet people, read interesting stories, or see video clips.
- Problem solving—it can help them find answers to a problem they have.
- Communication—it can be a way to send and receive messages.

KEY VERSE: *Wise people treasure knowledge, but the babbling of a fool invites trouble. (Proverbs 10:14)*

RELATED VERSES: *Proverbs 15:14; 18:15; 27:20; Ecclesiastes 12:12; 1 John 2:16*

RELATED QUESTIONS: *Why do people get on the Internet? What does it mean to "surf" with a computer?*

Q: IS THE INTERNET BAD?

76

A: The Internet itself is not bad. It is just like any other tool, such as a hammer, a book, or a phone—it can be used for both good and bad. Almost anything can be used this way, even things that are usually used for good. A hammer can be used to build a house or hurt someone. So the Internet can be misused and used for bad purposes, just as it can be used for good purposes. Sadly, some people do use it the bad way.

By itself, the Internet is just a very big network of networks. Whether it is used for good or for bad is up to us. It has great potential for good. We each need to do our part and use it right—to the glory of God.

KEY VERSE: *Whatever you eat or drink or whatever you do, you must do all for the glory of God. (1 Corinthians 10:31)*

RELATED VERSES: *1 Corinthians 10:30-33*

RELATED QUESTIONS: *Who invented the Internet? Why are there bad pictures on the Internet? What are tele-communications? How much does the Internet cost?*

Q: HOW COME THE OLDEN DAYS AND THESE DAYS ARE DIFFERENT?

77

A: First, people change the way they dress, the style of their homes, and the kinds of foods they eat. Second, and more importantly, technology keeps changing. Every year, engineers and inventors create new products and new ways of doing things. Some of these things can improve our lives, and others make things a little harder, but all of them bring change.

After the automobile was invented and became common, people didn't have to ride horses or horse-drawn buggies to travel from town to town. That was a huge change. And just think of the changes that came from airplanes, telephones, microwave ovens, antibiotics, vaccines, and computers. Then microphones, televisions, tape players, CD players, VCRs, and CD-ROM drives sure changed entertainment. Not that long ago, people didn't have any of these inventions.

But even with all the changes, many things stay the same. Human nature is the same—people still struggle and search for God. People still laugh and cry, and are born young and grow old. A year is still 365 days, people still have to work, and each person still needs God's love and lordship. And everyone still dies.

KEY VERSE: *Don't long for "the good old days," for you don't know whether they were any better than today.* *(Ecclesiastes 7:10)*

RELATED QUESTIONS: *In olden days, did they have phones? How come TV used to be black and white? Who invented electricity? Who invented TV? What is satellite TV?*

MEDICINE

Q: WHY DO PEOPLE GET SICK WHEN GOD IS WATCHING OVER THEM?

I THINK I HAVE A FLU BUG.

SNUFFLE SNUFFLE

BUG SPRAY

BUG SPRAY

78

A: Sickness was not part of God's original plan for us. We have sickness in the world because sin brought it in. As long as we live in this world, we will have sickness. God does not promise that he will keep all pain and sickness away from us, although he does promise to always be with us.

We need to take care of ourselves and guard against sickness by eating the right foods, getting enough sleep, and exercising. When we do get sick, we should take our medicine exactly as the doctor says and pray and ask God to help us recover.

Ecclesiastes 7:14 says, "Enjoy prosperity while you can. But when hard times strike, realize that both come from God."

In heaven God will end all sickness. This life is not all there is. Don't forget about heaven.

KEY VERSE: *Our bodies now disappoint us, but when they are raised, they will be full of glory. They are weak now, but when they are raised, they will be full of power. (1 Corinthians 15:43)*

RELATED VERSES: *Psalm 41:3; Romans 8:18-25; 2 Corinthians 12:8-10; James 5:14-15; Revelation 21:4*

RELATED QUESTIONS: *If God is watching over you, why do you still get the flu? How do you get diabetes? How do people get cancer? How does cancer start? How does asthma start? How do appendixes bust? How do you get constipated?*

79

A: When a person feels sick, that person's body is telling him or her that something is wrong. Pain and sick feelings can be a friend, an alarm system that alerts us to problems. Without these feelings, we would not know that something is wrong and that we need to do something about it (for example, eat certain foods, take medicine, or have an operation). People who don't have those bad feelings can hurt themselves more by not taking care of the problem.

KEY VERSES: *You guided my conception and formed me in the womb. You clothed me with skin and flesh, and you knit my bones and sinews together. (Job 10:10-11)*

RELATED VERSES: *Psalm 25:16-18; Revelation 21:4*

RELATED QUESTIONS: *How does your body feel that it's sick? How does your body get sick? Why do you get airsick?*

Q: WHAT ARE BACTERIA AND VIRUSES?

80

A: Bacteria are one-celled living things; viruses are parasites that attack living things. Both are so small that you need a microscope to see them. Harmful bacteria and viruses are often called germs. Germs make you sick by reproducing inside your body.

Bacteria are not always harmful. E. coli bacteria live in your intestines and help your body break down food. Several kinds of bacteria live in the ground and break up dead leaves, sticks, grass, and other organic matter to make compost. These bacteria could make you sick if they got on your food, but they serve a good purpose in nature.

Other bacteria are very harmful; streptococcus bacteria, for example, cause strep throat, a sickness that children and adults sometimes get. Doctors treat it with antibiotics, medicines that kill bacteria.

Bacteria and viruses are everywhere, but God made our bodies to fight them off. He gave us white blood cells and antibodies. These are your body's way of staying well and of curing itself of sickness.

KEY VERSE: *Thank you for making me so wonderfully complex! Your workmanship is marvelous—and how well I know it. (Psalm 139:14)*

RELATED VERSES: *James 5:14-15*

RELATED QUESTIONS: *What are viruses? How do you get viruses? Why do people spread germs so fast and why are they so rude about it?*

Q: WHY DO DOCTORS GIVE SOME SHOTS THAT ARE LONG AND SOME THAT ARE SHORT?

81

A: Doctors give different kinds of shots for different reasons. If the doctor uses a long needle, it is because he or she needs to get the medicine deep into your body so it can do its work. Doctors are trained to know what kind of shots to give. It's a matter of using the treatment that fits what you need. God grants doctors the wisdom they need to treat their patients with skill.

Of course, doctors don't know everything, but God does. You can ask him to give your doctor wisdom and help him or her to do an even better job.

KEY VERSE: *Wounds from a friend are better than many kisses from an enemy. (Proverbs 27:6)*

RELATED VERSES: *Proverbs 17:22; Matthew 9:12; James 5:14-15*

RELATED QUESTIONS: *Why do we have to have needles for shots? How come you get measles shots and booster shots? Why do you get a shot before you get a cast?*

NOTE TO PARENTS: *You can pray with your children before going to the doctor to help teach them that we still depend on God for our health. The Designer and Manufacturer knows more than the repair person, and he wants us to come to him with our needs.*

Q: WHY ARE DOCTORS SO SMART?

82

A: God makes every person with talents and abilities. He makes each person unique—one person has this skill, and another person has that skill. People who become doctors have the talents and abilities to do what doctors do.

But people aren't born being doctors. They have to get a lot of training. They have to go to school for a long time and study hard. They have to learn from other doctors who have a lot of experience. Only after they have done all that are they "so smart." They know a lot because they've learned a lot.

KEY VERSE: *Bezalel, Oholiab, and the other craftsmen whom the Lord has gifted with wisdom, skill, and intelligence will construct and furnish the Tabernacle, just as the Lord has commanded. (Exodus 36:1)*

RELATED VERSES: *Exodus 35:31-36; Proverbs 2:6; 17:24; 24:3-4*

RELATED QUESTIONS: *What if the doctors give a person the wrong medicine? Why do people buy medications when they don't need them?*

HOW DOES MEDICINE MAKE SOMEONE BETTER?

83

A: Medicine helps your body heal itself. Some medicines do this by killing germs; antibiotics work that way. Some medicines help the body do what it does even better. Some medicines stop the body from doing what it should not do; some asthma medicines work that way. Doctors often know what medicines to give for each sickness. The purpose of medicine is to help your body do the healing work.

The one thing medicine cannot do is heal your attitude. You can be cured of an illness but remain angry, selfish, and bitter. Or you may not be cured physically but still be thankful, peaceful, and trusting of God. It is important to place your hope and trust in God, no matter how sick you may be. That is what Job did.

In the end, it is God who heals people. God gives us our bodies and gives us the substances that make medicines work.

KEY VERSE: *Then Isaiah said to Hezekiah's servants, "Make an ointment from figs and spread it over the boil." They did this, and Hezekiah recovered! (2 Kings 20:7)*

RELATED VERSES: *Job 2:1-10; Psalm 103:2-3; Proverbs 18:14*

RELATED QUESTIONS: *How do you make medications? How does medicine work? How do "puffers" prevent asthma? How do glasses work?*

Q: WHO INVENTED VEGETABLES?

84

A: God created vegetables—they were his idea.
Our bodies need certain kinds of food, just as
a car needs a certain kind of fuel. You wouldn't put
hamburgers into a gas tank, would you? God gave us
vegetables as good food for us because that's one kind of
fuel our bodies need.

In fact, vegetables have several very important jobs.
First, they provide vitamins and minerals that help us
grow and become strong and healthy. Without these
vitamins and minerals, our body would not work right.
Vegetables also give us fiber, which is the part of plant
cells that your body cannot digest. Fiber carries all the
other foods through your digestive system. That may
sound unimportant, but without fiber, all the other food
you eat would get stuck in your digestive tract.

God gave us fruits and vegetables to eat so that our
bodies would work properly.

KEY VERSE: *"Test us for ten days on a diet of vegetables and water,"* *Daniel said. (Daniel 1:12)*

RELATED VERSES: *Genesis 1:29; Psalm 104:24*

RELATED QUESTIONS: *Why do parents make you eat tomatoes and onions when you don't want to eat them? How are vegetables good for us? Why are vegetables green?*

Q: WHY IS IT GOOD TO EXERCISE?

85

A: Your body needs exercise, just as it needs food, air, and water. Muscles need to be stretched and strengthened. The lungs need to breathe fresh, clean air. Joints need to be moved around. Blood needs to get moving. Exercise is a way of taking care of your body. Exercise also helps people lose weight by using the food, building muscle, and burning fat.

Some people today don't get enough exercise—they sit around watching TV, playing video games, or surfing the Internet for a long time. Sitting around all the time is not good for a person's health. You need to get out and use your body. Good exercise comes from working around the house, working in the yard, riding bikes, running, walking, and playing sports.

God gave us wonderful bodies, and he wants us to take care of them. And we all need exercise to do that properly.

KEY VERSE: *Physical exercise has some value, but spiritual exercise is much more important, for it promises a reward in both this life and the next. (1 Timothy 4:8)*

RELATED VERSES: *1 Corinthians 6:19-20; 1 Timothy 5:23*

RELATED QUESTIONS: *How does exercise help lose weight? How does exercising make you lose weight? How come people make machines that make you lose weight?*

Q: WHY DO PEOPLE SMOKE?

86

A: People smoke because they are addicted to the nicotine in the cigarettes. Nicotine is a chemical in tobacco. Once you start putting nicotine into your body, your body starts to crave it. You start to feel like you *need* it. Smoking gives your body the nicotine it craves, and this makes it hard to stop.

People also get addicted to the experience. That is, they get used to having a cigarette at certain times of the day. It becomes a habit.

Most people who smoke started when they were very young. They may have started because they thought that smoking would make them look cool or tough or because they liked the taste. Maybe someone they knew talked them into it. After a while, however, they got tired of smoking—it's not cool anymore. But they have become addicted to the nicotine and find it almost impossible to stop.

It is important for us to take good care of our body. Smoking damages many parts of our body. God didn't make our lungs to breathe in smoke.

Try not to be too hard on people who smoke. Quitting is very difficult.

KEY VERSES: *I don't understand myself at all, for I really want to do what is right, but I don't do it. Instead, I do the very thing I hate. I know perfectly well that what I am doing is wrong, and my bad conscience shows that I agree that the law is good. But I can't help myself, because it is sin inside me that makes me do these evil things. (Romans 7:15-17)*

RELATED VERSES: *Matthew 7:1-6; 1 Corinthians 6:19-20; Galatians 5:22-24*

RELATED QUESTIONS: *Why is smoking bad for you? Does smoking make your lungs gross?*

Q: WHAT DOES CLONING MEAN?

87

A: Cloning means making an exact copy of a living thing's DNA, or genetic code. It involves taking the genetic code of a plant or animal and making another plant or animal from that code. Cloning bypasses the usual means of reproduction from a male and female. It's like making a photocopy of a living plant or animal, or building two houses with the same measurements.

Cloning does *not* mean making an exact copy of a person. Cloning copies only the *body,* not the soul, the spirit, or the experiences that also make a person who he or she is. Even if someone could make an exact physical copy of your eyes, knees, and brain, the clone would still be different from you. Your personality, experiences, desires, dreams, choices, and relationship with God would all be different from the clone's. It is all of these things together that make you one of a kind.

No one could ever be exactly like you. Isn't that great?

KEY VERSE: *You made all the delicate, inner parts of my body and knit me together in my mother's womb. (Psalm 139:13)*

RELATED VERSES: *Psalm 139:13-16*

RELATED QUESTIONS: *Is cloning going to happen to all animals? How do you clone someone? Why do people argue over medical ethics? What are medical ethics? Can scientists create life in a test tube? Is the life they create in a test tube like a blob or virus?*

Q: WHY DOES GOD LET PEOPLE DIE?

LIAR

LIAR

LIA

LIAR

SNAKE EXHIBIT

88

A: People die because sin came into the world when Adam and Eve sinned. In fact, everyone dies eventually. Some people die when they're young, some die when they're old, and some die when they're in the prime of life. But no matter how long a person lives, his or her life sooner or later comes to an end.

God can heal people and stop them from dying, and sometimes he does. But even a person who has been healed through a miracle from God will die someday.

But God's people know that death is not the end of the story. This life is *not* all there is. People who know God will go to live with him in heaven after they die. So it is very important for us to be ready to meet him when we die.

KEY VERSE: *For we know that when this earthly tent we live in is taken down—when we die and leave these bodies— we will have a home in heaven, an eternal body made for us by God himself and not by human hands. (2 Corinthians 5:1)*

RELATED VERSES: *Romans 8:38-39; 1 Corinthians 15:35-58; 2 Corinthians 5:1-8; Revelation 21:4*

RELATED QUESTION: *Why do children die?*

OUTER SPACE

Q: WHY IS THERE A UNIVERSE?

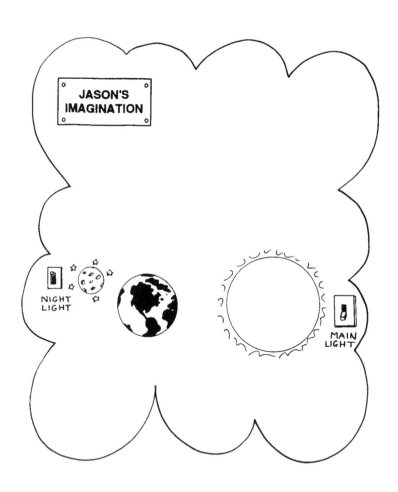

89

A: *Universe* is another word for the creation—everything that God created. God created it all. He created every star, every galaxy, every black hole, every atom. And God created everything very good. We don't know why God created everything in the universe, but we do know that he had a good reason.

We also know that God designed the universe for us to live in. The Bible says that God placed the stars and the moon in the night sky to give us light during the night, and the sun to give us light during the day. God had us in mind when he created these things; he gave them their design so that we could live on this earth. They are a sign of God's care and love for us.

The Bible also says that the creation is evidence of God's existence (see Romans 1:20). When people look around and see the earth and all the stars, they know that these things came from God.

KEY VERSE: *By faith we understand that the entire universe was formed at God's command, that what we now see did not come from anything that can be seen. (Hebrews 11:3)*

RELATED VERSES: *Genesis 1:16-18; John 1:3; Romans 1:20; Colossians 1:16-17*

RELATED QUESTIONS: *Why does the world spin around? How fast does the sun travel? How far is Pluto from the sun? Why is there a ring around Saturn? How many moons are there in space? Why is our galaxy called the Milky Way?*

NOTE TO PARENTS: *Creation tells us something about God's power and nature. You can look out at the night sky with your children and talk about what the stars tell us about God.*

Q: IS OUTER SPACE HOT OR COLD?

90

A: Most of outer space is very cold; only the stars and the space right around them are hot. God created the universe with over a billion billion stars. The stars put out a lot of heat, but there is a lot more space than stars. So anything not close to a star has almost no heat at all. The heat produced by the Sun, the star that's closest to Earth, produces just the right amount of light and heat for us to live on our planet. The air on Earth keeps the heat in. God created the earth with just the right climate so that human beings, his special creations, could live here. Earth is our home.

KEY VERSES: *When I look at the night sky and see the work of your fingers—the moon and the stars you have set in place—what are mortals that you should think of us, mere humans that you should care for us? (Psalm 8:3-4)*

RELATED VERSES: *Psalm 33:6; Proverbs 3:19-20; Colossians 1:15-17*

RELATED QUESTIONS: *How come it's cold in space? Why did God make so many different planets?*

Q: WHY DO PEOPLE WANT TO FLY TO OTHER PLANETS?

COLLECTING FOR NASA'S
SPACE STATION

91

A: Some people want to travel to other planets because they want to know how the universe began. Even those who believe that God created everything are curious about how he did it. The stars, the planets, and all the universe are marvelous displays of God's handiwork.

Other people are simply curious. They want to travel to other planets to see them up close, to see what it would be like to go there, and to learn all they can. It would certainly be an adventure!

KEY VERSE: *It is God's privilege to conceal things and the king's privilege to discover them. (Proverbs 25:2)*

RELATED VERSES: *Psalm 19:1-6; Proverbs 25:3*

RELATED QUESTIONS: *How come astronauts went up to outer space to find planets? Why do people want to build settlements on other planets? How would people get oxygen if they lived on Mars? How would people get supplies up to Mars? Why do some people think there is life on Mars? How would little germs or worms survive on Mars? How would life on Mars live without oxygen?*

Q: IF THERE'S INTELLIGENT LIFE ON OTHER PLANETS, DO THEY HAVE TEACHERS?

92

A: The universe is so big that we can't even imagine how big it is. The nearest star, Alpha Centauri, is 25 *trillion* miles from our sun, and Alpha Centauri has no planets. It is possible that God created life on other planets, far, far away. But we don't know anything about that because we have no evidence for other living beings on other planets. And even if we could travel at the speed of light, which is over 600 million miles per hour, it would take us over four years just to go to Alpha Centauri. Unless we invent some form of space travel that takes us across the galaxy faster than light, we will probably never know whether God created life on other planets. Only God knows exactly what he created far out in space.

KEY VERSE: *The Lord merely spoke, and the heavens were created. He breathed the word, and all the stars were born. (Psalm 33:6)*

RELATED VERSES: *Proverbs 3:19-20; 25:2-3; Colossians 1:15-17*

RELATED QUESTIONS: *Why do people think there is life on other planets? Are aliens smarter than earth people? Why do people think beings from other planets are smarter than earth people?*

Q: WHY DO PEOPLE THINK THAT BEINGS FROM OTHER PLANETS HAVE VISITED EARTH?

93

A: Some people believe that beings from other planets have visited earth. Here are some of the reasons they think so:

1. It would be exciting if it were true (wishful thinking).
2. It is one way people explain certain things that used to be hard to explain, such as how the pyramids in Egypt were built.
3. They know there is more to our existence than just ourselves, but they refuse to believe in God, so they look in outer space instead.
4. They want to connect to something that is beyond what they know or experience on earth.

Some people even think that human beings were put on earth by beings from outer space. They do not believe in God or that God created us, and this is the way they explain where we came from.

KEY VERSE: *It should be explained that all the Athenians as well as the foreigners in Athens seemed to spend all their time discussing the latest ideas. (Acts 17:21)*

RELATED VERSES: *Genesis 1:27; Psalm 8:3-8*

RELATED QUESTIONS: *Why do people want to know if there's life on other planets? Is there life on other planets? Are aliens real?*

Q: WHY DO PEOPLE WANT TO LIVE ON THE MOON IF THEY WOULDN'T BE ABLE TO BREATHE THERE?

94

A: The main reason for living on the moon would be for learning—studying astronomy and trying to understand the universe better. Some people want to go to the moon to mine it. Some just want to travel and explore.

Few people really want to live on the moon, however, even if the trip were completely safe. It would cost an enormous amount of money to get there. There would be no trees, fresh air, streams, or other things to enjoy. It would also be very difficult to live and to get around. Again, the main reason for going would be to study and do research.

KEY VERSE: *Intelligent people are always open to new ideas. In fact, they look for them. (Proverbs 18:15)*

RELATED VERSES: *Deuteronomy 4:19; Psalm 74:16-17; Proverbs 25:2; Isaiah 45:18; Jeremiah 31:35*

RELATED QUESTIONS: *How can you breathe in outer space? Do they have medicine for people who get hurt up in space? How do they make astronaut suits? How many people have gone to the moon?*

Q: HOW DO PEOPLE THINK OF THINGS LIKE THE HUBBLE TELESCOPE?

95

A: People who invent marvelous instruments like the Hubble telescope are very talented and intelligent people. God gave them the brains and ability to think of such things. God let them learn and develop the skills to make their inventions. They read, investigated, learned, and studied hard for a long time. The skills and knowledge that people like that use to create such amazing tools come from God, and those people have used them well.

It is a beautiful part of human nature to be able to create and invent things that are useful to us. It is a part of God's image in us. It is a part of God's image in you.

KEY VERSE: *For you made us only a little lower than God, and you crowned us with glory and honor. (Psalm 8:5)*

RELATED VERSES: *Genesis 1:27; Job 38:36; Proverbs 3:13, 19*

RELATED QUESTIONS: *How far can the Hubble telescope see? How do people get the pictures from the Hubble telescope? Why don't they bring the Hubble telescope back down to Earth?*

Q: CAN KIDS BE ASTRONAUTS IF THEY GET TRAINED?

96

A: Kids can't be astronauts because it takes so long to train for it. It takes many years of training and conditioning to withstand the rigors of space flight. Your body has to be in top shape and strong. Even if a young person were chosen to be an astronaut, he or she would be quite a bit older at the end of the training. So you might say that a kid can't be an astronaut, but a kid can train to become an astronaut when he or she is older.

Very few people actually become astronauts, although thousands try. Only the very best get chosen.

KEY VERSES: *Remember that in a race everyone runs, but only one person gets the prize. You also must run in such a way that you will win. All athletes practice strict self-control. They do it to win a prize that will fade away, but we do it for an eternal prize. (1 Corinthians 9:24-25)*

RELATED VERSES: *Luke 2:39-40; 1 Corinthians 13:11; 1 Timothy 4:12*

RELATED QUESTIONS: *I know astronauts have to go through training, but can't kids go to space if they get trained? Why aren't children allowed to be astronauts? What if they were trained?*

NOTE TO PARENTS: *Whenever your children are interested in doing something difficult with their life, try not to discourage them from trying just because it takes a lot of effort. Instead, encourage their vision, pray with them about it, and let them know what they have to do to get there.*

THE
BEGINNING
AND
THE END

Q: WHY DID GOD CREATE THE WORLD?

97

A: God has not told us exactly why he created the world. We know that God enjoys making things, and that he wanted to be with us. God created people because he wanted to have friends—men and women, boys and girls with whom he could share his love. He created the world for us to live in and enjoy. God loves us. Perhaps that is all the reason he needed.

KEY VERSE: *For the Lord is God, and he created the heavens and earth and put everything in place. He made the world to be lived in, not to be a place of empty chaos. "I am the Lord," he says, "and there is no other." (Isaiah 45:18)*

RELATED VERSES: *Genesis 1:1; Psalm 148:5-6; John 1:1-14; 3:16; Acts 17:27; Colossians 1:15-17*

RELATED QUESTIONS: *How come God created the earth? Why did God rest on the seventh day? What is the big bang theory?*

Q: HOW WAS GOD CREATED?

SPEED OF LIGHT × GALACTIC
GRAVITATIONAL TRIANGULATION
(12 × escape velocity) +
SUB-MOLECULAR INFUSION
DIFFUSION INVERSION
CAPACITY ÷ 732.98702
PER ANNUM + ETERNITY FACTOR

= GOD HAS ALWAYS EXISTED

98

A: God was not created; he has always existed. This is impossible for us to understand because everything else we know about has a beginning and an end. But God had no beginning, and he has no end. He always was, and he always will be.

Imagine going on a deep-sea dive and being able to talk to the fish at the bottom of the sea. Imagine trying to explain to the fish what life is like for humans above the surface of the water and on land. The fish would not be able to understand, no matter how hard you tried to explain it. Everything he knows is in the water. *You* can breathe air and walk on the land, but the fish knows nothing about that. So the fish thinks it's silly or impossible.

That is the way it is with God. God created everything we know, including time. Beginnings and endings are limitations of our world, but not of God. That is one of the great things about him—he is so much greater than we are!

KEY VERSES: *In the beginning the Word already existed. He was with God, and he was God. He was in the beginning with God. He created everything there is. Nothing exists that he didn't make. (John 1:1-3)*

RELATED VERSES: *Exodus 3:14; Revelation 1:8; 4:8-11; 5:14*

RELATED QUESTIONS: *How did God get made? Why do people think God has a white beard and is sitting on a throne in heaven?*

Q: WHY DO SOME PEOPLE BELIEVE THAT HUMANS CAME FROM MONKEYS?

99

A: Many people today believe that human beings descended from apelike creatures millions of years ago. In other words, they believe that way, way back in time certain animals changed so that they eventually became human. This is known as the theory of evolution.

There are three main reasons that people believe this: (1) They prefer *not* to believe that God created Adam and Eve and that all people descended from those two people, so they need another explanation. (2) Many scientists tell us that the theory of evolution explains the fossil record. Therefore, it seems reasonable to people. (3) So many *other* people believe the theory of evolution that they assume it must be true.

The Bible teaches, however, that God created human beings at a certain time and that he created them "in his own image" (Genesis 1:27). This means that humans are not just smart animals. Every human being is a special creation of God. The Bible also says that only God was witness to creation.

KEY VERSE: *So God created people in his own image; God patterned them after himself; male and female he created them. (Genesis 1:27)*

RELATED VERSES: *Job 38:1–40:1; Revelation 4:11*

RELATED QUESTIONS: *If we come from monkeys, where did monkeys come from? What is evolution? What's the theory of evolution? How do we know that everything didn't evolve?*

NOTE TO PARENTS: *Evolution is merely a theory—one way of explaining the past. Many textbooks and teachers today present it as fact, but it is not. Explain this to your children so they will be prepared for discussions in school.*

Q: CAN YOU FIGURE OUT HOW OLD THE EARTH IS BY YOURSELF?

100

A: No. Scientists have come up with ways to figure out how old the world is, but no one can know for sure whether these ways are true, and it is impossible to test them because no one can go back in time. There is no book that tells about everything that happened since the creation of the earth. Not even the Bible has an unbroken record of history. Many people think that the earth is billions of years old; others think it is much younger. But no one really knows how old the earth is, and there is no foolproof way to find out.

What we do know is this: God created Adam and Eve and all life on earth many thousands of years ago. It was not an accident or a product of time—it was God's doing.

KEY VERSES: *Where were you when I laid the foundations of the earth? Tell me, if you know so much. Do you know how its dimensions were determined and who did the surveying? What supports its foundations, and who laid its cornerstone as the morning stars sang together and all the angels shouted for joy? (Job 38:4-7)*

RELATED VERSES: *Genesis 1:1-31; Job 38:8-30; John 1:3; Colossians 1:16*

RELATED QUESTIONS: *Does the Bible actually say how old the world is? How old is the world?*

101

A: Some people say the world is getting overpopulated, but it is not true. There is plenty of room for everyone. It is true that many *cities* have too many people. In fact, in some places thousands of poor people live in an area that is much too small for them. And in some areas people do not get enough food. But the world itself has enough room for everyone, and it has enough farmland to grow food for everyone too.

Selfishness is a bigger problem than the threat of overpopulation. If people would help each other and always be kind to each other, hunger and overcrowding would not be so much of a problem.

KEY VERSES: *Children are a gift from the Lord; they are a reward from him. Children born to a young man are like sharp arrows in a warrior's hands. How happy is the man whose quiver is full of them! He will not be put to shame when he confronts his accusers at the city gates. (Psalm 127:3-5)*

RELATED VERSES: *Genesis 1:28; Proverbs 11:25; Acts 2:44-45*

RELATED QUESTIONS: *How many people should there be on earth? How come people think the world is overpopulated? Is it all right if you have 4 billion people on earth?*

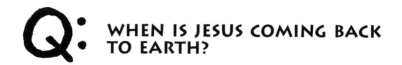

Q: WHEN IS JESUS COMING BACK TO EARTH?

102

A: When Jesus ascended into heaven, angels promised that he would return, just as he said. But Jesus said that he would return when people least expect it. So no one knows exactly when he is coming back. It could be today; it could be far, far in the future.

That is why Jesus told us to be ready for his return all the time. We should stay close to God and always do what is right.

Although no one knows when Jesus will return, we do know that every day brings his return closer. And when he comes, it will be a wonderful day for those who love him. He will create a new heaven and a new earth where his people will live with him forever. He will put an end to all evil, suffering, pain, and death. And we will get to be with friends and family who love Jesus, all happier than we can possibly imagine now.

KEY VERSES: *However, no one knows the day or hour when these things will happen, not even the angels in heaven or the Son himself. Only the Father knows. And since you don't know when they will happen, stay alert and keep watch. (Mark 13:32-33)*

RELATED VERSES: *1 Corinthians 15:51-58; 1 Thessalonians 4:15–5:11; 2 Thessalonians 1:7-10; 2:1-6*

RELATED QUESTIONS: *Is God really going to come back to earth? How come Jesus didn't say when he was coming back? Why do people think that God will come back? Could Jesus come back right now? Why will nonbelievers be afraid when Jesus comes back? Why isn't God coming back right now?*

Q: HOW IS GOD ALWAYS THERE?

103

A: God can always be with us because he does not have a physical body. God does not have to stay in one place the way we do. We don't know exactly how this works, but that's OK. God is much, much greater and more amazing than we can imagine. Isn't it great to know that God is there . . . and here?

KEY VERSE: *Teach these new disciples to obey all the commands I have given you. And be sure of this: I am with you always, even to the end of the age. (Matthew 28:20)*

RELATED VERSES: *Psalm 46:1; 139:7-12; John 14:16-17*

RELATED QUESTION: *How can God see everything?*

Q: HOW WILL THE WORLD END?

104

A: We don't know exactly *how* the world will end, but we know that it *will* end—the world will not go on forever. This is not bad news; it is part of God's plan. The world will not be destroyed by people or by things getting out of control. It will be God's doing and in God's timing. It will end in a blaze of fire! God will replace this world with a new one.

But it will not happen until Jesus comes back. He will return, just as he promised, to judge all people who have ever lived and to set up his kingdom. He will replace our damaged world with a new, perfect one, where his people will live with him forever. For those who love him, the end of the world will really be a beginning—a wonderful, awesome beginning!

KEY VERSE: *Then I saw a new heaven and a new earth, for the old heaven and the old earth had disappeared. And the sea was also gone. (Revelation 21:1)*

RELATED VERSES: *2 Peter 3:7; Revelation 21:1–22:6*

RELATED QUESTION: *Is the end of the world ever going to happen?*

Q: WHY DOES ETERNITY LAST FOR A LONG, LONG, LONG, LONG TIME?

THEORY OF ETERNITY

x + y² - sleeps - winks + time spent - blinks and lost time < time standing still + .002 and + xyz pie + infinity + kazillion and 1 kajillion = ETERNITY (approximately)

105

A: It doesn't. It lasts forever, and that's longer than a long time. That's what the word *eternity* means—"infinite or endless time."

It is impossible for people to understand eternity. It's beyond what our brain can imagine, because everything we imagine has limits. But God knows because he has no limits, and he is eternal.

KEY VERSE: *God has made everything beautiful for its own time. He has planted eternity in the human heart, but even so, people cannot see the whole scope of God's work from beginning to end. (Ecclesiastes 3:11)*

RELATED VERSES: *Psalm 119:89-90; Isaiah 26:4; Daniel 4:34; John 3:16; Revelation 7:12*

RELATED QUESTION: *How do I understand eternity?*

Q: IF THE BIBLE SAYS WE'LL LIVE FOR ETERNITY, WHY IS THERE AN END ON EARTH?

A:

The earth was not made to last forever. Things only last forever if God wants them to. God has determined that the world the way it is now will be destroyed and then made new again. God will give us a new heaven and a new earth to replace the old one. The new earth will be perfect in every way, as God intended it to be.

But people *will* last forever. When Jesus returns to make the world new, he will judge every person who has ever lived. Those who have received his forgiveness will be welcomed into his home, to live with him forever. And those who have refused his forgiveness will be cast into the lake of fire. That is why Jesus came, "so that everyone who believes in him will not perish but have eternal life" (see John 3:16).

KEY VERSES: *For all creation is waiting eagerly for that future day when God will reveal who his children really are. Against its will, everything on earth was subjected to God's curse. All creation anticipates the day when it will join God's children in glorious freedom from death and decay. For we know that all creation has been groaning as in the pains of childbirth right up to the present time. (Romans 8:19-22)*

RELATED VERSES: *Matthew 25:46; John 3:16; 2 Peter 3:7; Jude 1:14-15; Revelation 21:1*

RELATED QUESTIONS: *Will we all be adults in heaven? Why is there an end of the world anyway; can't it go on forever? Why do people say that the end of the world is coming? Would anybody be living at the end of the world?*